D1095296

DISORDERED BEHAVIOR

BASIC CONCEPTS IN CLINICAL PSYCHIATRY

Disordered Behavior

BASIC CONCEPTS IN CLINICAL PSYCHIATRY

ERIC PFEIFFER, M.D.
Assistant Professor of Psychiatry
Duke University Medical Center
Durham, North Carolina

New York

OXFORD UNIVERSITY PRESS 1968

London Toronto

THIS BOOK IS DEDICATED TO
MY SON *Eric Alexander*

Preface

This book is intended as an introduction to clinical psychiatry, and was originally addressed to medical students exclusively. As the writing progressed, however, it became apparent that the material being presented had interest and value to a much wider audience, one that included students of social work, of nursing, and of abnormal psychology, teachers and clergymen, and last, but perhaps most important, those informal students of human behavior, intelligent readers in general.

This book is not a textbook in the usual sense of the word. The major themes and clinical syndromes in psychiatry are presented, but no attempt has been made to be encyclopedic. Instead, proper emphasis is given to conditions which occur commonly, leaving for more specialized study the more esoteric concepts and conditions in this field.

It has been assumed that the reader already has a speaking acquaintance with basic psychological and biological concepts, in particular, with child development, adaptation, communication, and interpersonal and intrapersonal conflict on the psychological side, and with basic brain functioning on the biological side. (Where this assumption is not true, the reader is referred to George Engel's excellent book *Psychological Development in Health and Disease*, Saunders, 1962.)

Psychiatry is a clinical specialty in which many differing points of view prevail. What is presented in this book is *not a new point of view but a new integration* of many differing points of view.

While much of what is contained in these pages is derived from published books and articles and from the teachings of my teachers and colleagues, I must take sole responsibility for the particular synthesis presented here, for better or worse.

E. P.

Durham, N.C.
November 1967

Contents

DISORDERED BEHAVIOR

BASIC CONCEPTS IN CLINICAL PSYCHIATRY

1

Introduction

Clinical psychiatry is a specialized branch of medicine. It deals with the study and treatment of *disordered behavior.* We prefer the term "disordered behavior" to the term "mental diseases" because the latter implies that there are actual disease states of the mind which are analogous to bodily disease states. This notion, once widely held, is no longer generally accepted. It developed at a time when man was thought of dualistically, that is, as composed of two separate entities, body and mind. Today man is more often viewed monistically, that is, as an organismic whole, whose mental and physical functions are seen as differing yet never entirely separable attributes of the same, integrated being.

Some of the clinical problems with which psychiatrists deal are caused by structural, physiological, or biochemical changes in the brain. These disorders correspond closely to what is generally regarded as "disease," although they are not so much "mental diseases" as they are "brain diseases." Psychiatrists also deal with patients, far greater in number than those mentioned above, whose behavior is disordered, but who do not show evidence of any recognizable organic disease process. Here two explanations are possible: (a) Organic brain disturbances do in fact exist, but are of such subtle nature that present methodology does not permit us to recognize them. (b) No biochemical or structural brain disturbances exist; instead, the disordered behavior is due to faulty or unfortunate learning and life experiences, to "faulty

3

programming," as it were. Such disorders, too, are not so much "mental diseases" as they are "problems of adaptation" or "problems in living." Problems in adaptation *and* brain diseases with behavioral manifestations fall within the province of clinical psychiatry.

In using the term "disordered behavior" we can include for study, without prejudice or initial regard as to the causal factors involved, disorganized, maladaptive, disturbed, and disturbing behavior. In studying individual instances of disordered behavior, however, we must make a careful assessment of the factors responsible for the specific difficulties experienced. It is not sufficient to determine whether the causes are primarily organic or primarily experiential. We must go further and determine *the specific organic and experiential factors, the relative contribution of each, and the interactions between them.*

The Tools of the Psychiatrist

Psychiatrists make use of tools and techniques of evaluation and treatment which are similar to those used by other medical specialists. But in addition, and to a far greater extent, they apply psychological or psychosocial methods and principles which differ significantly from those used in general medicine. In the *medical* approach, *evaluation leads to the diagnosis of one or more diseases;* in the *psychosocial* approach, *evaluation leads to an understanding of the individual patient.* In the *medical* model, *the aim of treatment is eradication or control of a disease process;* in the *psychosocial* model, *it is re-education of the patient.*

How, then, do psychiatrists gain an understanding of their patients? How do they treat or re-educate their patients? The second question will be dealt with throughout the book, but particularly in the chapter on psychotherapy. To the first question, however, we will try to provide an answer here. Psychiatrists come to understand their patients not by looking at them with a magnifying glass or some highly technical instrument but *by in-* *teracting with them, by listening to them.*

Freud recommended listening to patients with what he called an "evenly-hovering attention," a frame of mind which is alert to the details of the moment-to-moment interaction between doctor and patient *and* to the over-all pattern of the patient's psychological functioning (1). Reik, a sometime student of Freud, expanded this concept by focusing not only on what the patient did, said, and felt, but also on what the psychiatrist did, said, and felt while interacting with his patient. He called this, somewhat poetically, "listening with the third ear," with an inner ear as it were (2). Sullivan, too, made it clear, that listening to patients was not a one-way interaction when he labeled the process of psychotherapy as one of "participant observation" (3). All three of these authors agree that the tools of the psychiatrist are his own faculties, his own personality.

Empathy

One of the most important of these faculties is empathy. It is not a faculty which psychiatrists alone possess; it is a common human faculty. It is the means by which strangers can understand one another, the means by which psychiatrists can understand the seemingly strange behavior of their patients. It is based on the assumption that "we are all much more simply human than otherwise," as Sullivan put it (3). That is to say, the areas of communality of human experience are far more impressive than the areas of individual differences between people.

The word "empathy" is a translation of the German word *Einfuehlung*. The term was first introduced by Lipps (4), a German psychologist and philosopher; it means "feeling oneself into another person" or "burrowing into another's feelings." It needs to be distinguished from sympathy, which literally means "feeling along with another" but which ordinarily is used only in the sense of compassion. Both empathy and compassion have uses in medical practice, as Aring has pointed out (5), but empathy is the more versatile of the two.

Empathy, as it is commonly practised between psychiatrist and patient, involves three fairly distinct steps: (a) a sampling of the thoughts and feelings of the patient by a process which we shall discuss further below—"How must it feel to be in his shoes?"; (b) an intellectual processing of the information gained by this sampling; (c) a response of some kind which indicates to the patient that the psychiatrist has in fact understood (6). The empathizer does not step into the other person's shoes and stay there. Nor does he take over the other person's feelings. He makes "reflective, not reflexive" judgments about another person's problems, keeping separate his own and the other person's identity (5).

The phenomenon of empathy is still not thoroughly understood (7). It is particularly difficult to explain how it is possible to "sample" another person's feelings. This step involves a readiness on the part of the psychiatrist to permit himself to be momentarily, not enduringly, contaminated by the patient's feelings. Feelings are communicated primarily by non-verbal cues—by tone of voice, facial expressions, hand gestures, postures, and by distinctive combinations of all of these. By paying attention to these non-verbal as well as to the verbal communications, the psychiatrist can keep a running awareness of the feeling tone of his patient. We have spoken of a momentary contagion of feeling. The psychiatrist wants to experience just enough of the patient's feelings to be able to identify them but not be overwhelmed by them.

THE NEED TO BE UNDERSTOOD

We have throughout this chapter referred to the importance of understanding the patient. To be understood and accepted by one's fellow man is one of the major aims of human endeavor. Sullivan felt that psychiatric problems were far more often caused by failure to gain acceptance and understanding from other people (failure to achieve interpersonal security) than by failure to obtain full satisfaction of all one's biological needs (3).

What accounts for this human need to be accepted and understood by other people? We would say that *other people are important in later life because they are all-important in early life.* Human biology is such that we are born helpless, and that we continue helpless for an actually or proportionately longer period of time than any other animal. Survival depends on other people's understanding, accepting, and meeting our varying needs over a period of years. It should not be too surprising then that being understood, which has for so long been *associated* with the satisfaction of our biological needs, should eventually become a need in itself. This need rivals in magnitude any of the basic biological needs. Nor is a purely intellectual understanding, without emotional acceptance, enough. This is dramatically illustrated by a female patient who said of her husband: "The more I understood him, the more I disliked him."

In the chapters which follow we shall discuss some of the most frequently observed patterns of disordered behavior. Since this is a book on clinical psychiatry, we shall focus principally on abnormal behavior. But the reader should keep in mind that abnormal behavior constitutes only a small segment of the over-all functioning of most patients, and that disordered and smoothly functioning aspects of the personality co-exist. In regard to the particular pattern of disordered behavior, too, we need to say that this is not necessarily limited to one or another type in a given patient. The presence of certain kinds of problems and conflicts does not preclude the presence of others. It is the psychiatrist's job to determine not only which problems exist, but the degree to which each of them contributes to the patient's suffering.

REFERENCES

1. Sigmund Freud, "The Dynamics of the Transference," in *Collected Papers,* Vol. II, Basic Books, New York, 1959.

2. Theodore Reik, *Listening with the Third Ear,* Grove Press, New York, 1956.
3. Harry Stack Sullivan, *Conceptions of Modern Psychiatry,* William A. White Psychiatric Foundation, Washington, 1947.
4. Theodor Lipps, *Zur Einfuehlung,* W. Engelmann, Leipzig, 1913.
5. Charles D. Aring, "Sympathy and Empathy," *J.A.M.A.,* 167:448–52, 1958.
6. Eric Pfeiffer and Everett H. Ellinwood, Jr., "The Concept of Empathy," unpublished data.
7. Robert L. Katz, *Empathy; Its Nature and Uses,* Free Press of Glencoe, New York, 1963.

2

Affective Disorders

Human behavior, whether healthy or disturbed, is always of one piece, integrated, whole, and indivisible. For didactic and heuristic purposes, however, it is permissible to divide behavior into acting, thinking, and feeling. In this book we will discuss many types of psychiatric disorders. In some, thinking disturbances predominate (e.g. schizophrenia); in some, action is characteristically disturbed (e.g. psychopathic personality); in some, mood disturbances are the outstanding feature (affective disorders, see below); in still others, disturbances appear in all three areas, without any single one's being outstandingly hard hit.

In this chapter we will deal with the *affective disorders,* a group of disturbances characterized by major deviations of mood, usually in the direction of either depression or elation. In these disorders, disturbances of thought and of action also occur, but they are of lesser importance and are typically in congruence with the prevailing mood or affect.

Kraepelin in 1896 introduced the term *manic-depressive psychosis* to designate "on the one hand the whole domain of so-called periodic or circular insanity, on the other hand simple mania and the greater part of the morbid states termed melancholia." (1) This term is still in use today, sometimes narrowly defined and sometimes rather inclusively. We, however, prefer the term *affective disorders* for this class of disturbances, inasmuch as it is more

9

purely descriptive and less liable to misunderstanding. This term will be used throughout this book.

On the Episodic Nature of Affective Disturbances

To some degree, all mental disorder is episodic: phobias come and go, schizophrenic patients have exacerbations and remissions, and character problems are intermittently more or less troublesome. But affective disorders occupy a unique position in this regard. Manic and/or depressive illnesses have fairly clear-cut demarcations in time. They tend to have a definite onset, to run a definite course lasting from several weeks to several years, and then to remit, with or without treatment, leaving the individual no worse off than he was before the onset of the affective disturbance. This is in contrast to schizophrenia, in which fluctuations in symptomatology are much less regular and the statement that the illness "does not permit a full *restitutio ad integrum*" (restitution to integrity) forms part of at least one definition of that disorder (2).

We shall proceed by discussing first the major depressive reactions, then go on to the manic reactions. The minor depressive reactions, including neurotic depressions, the normative grief reactions, and reactions to physical illnesses, which will only be touched on in this section will be dealt with more fully elsewhere.

DEPRESSION

We begin with definitions. In the beginning, definitions are rarely satisfactory, and it is only as we come to use words that they assume for us a more limited, agreed-upon meaning. Thus the word "depression" in psychiatric usage denotes two distinct but related ideas: depression as affect; depression as a clinical state.

Depression as Affect

This is the broadest, most theoretical, most abstract use of the term depression. As used in this sense it is not tied to any clinical situation. It denotes depression as one of a class of qualitatively distinct feelings states, having its own biological roots, psychological determinants, subjective manifestations, and objective autonomic or physiognomic expression. It is of greater interest to the research scientist than to the clinician, and we will not deal with it in this book.

Depression as a Clinical State

Clinical states of depression can vary widely. They can be classified according to a number of criteria; motivational criteria, biological criteria, or purely descriptive criteria. One of the most reliable, although not universally accepted, methods of classifying depressive states, is according to their severity. In this we should recognize that quantitative increases, beyond a certain point, can amount to qualitative change. Using severity of depression as our criterion, we can recognize three meanings of the word depression. One, depression as a common, everyday feeling state. Everyone has experienced brief periods of dejection in response to life's stresses and minor disappointments. Often a series of minor reverses makes people feel temporarily sad, listless, and withdrawn. This may last for a few minutes or as long as a full day. These states are undoubtedly unpleasant and as such are of "clinical" interest. But people do not ordinarily seek psychiatric help for them, although they might seek out a trusted friend or engage in some other pleasurable activity that has cheered them in the past.

Two, depression as symptom or symptom complex. Used in this sense, depression means a more prolonged reaction to major reverses or disappointments in life such as the loss of a job, the death of a loved one, an unhappy love affair, or the occurrence of a major physical illness. It is characterized by a constellation of symptoms in which painful dejection or sadness is the major component. Such depressions have been variously called *reactive* or *neurotic* depressions; and when the loss has been a bereavement, the term *grief reaction* has been applied. Many, but by no means all, persons with such reaction patterns may seek psychiatric help, for this level of depression can significantly interfere with everyday functioning.

Three, "*definitive* depression." By this term we mean those major depressive reactions which are either so severe or which persist for such an inordinate length of time as to be altogether outside the range of common experience. Under this heading we include psychotic depressive reactions, manic-depressive reactions, and involutional psychotic reactions, as well as a cluster of less clearly delineated entities; schizo-affective disorders, postpartum depressions, and the major depressions of old age.

DEFINITIVE DEPRESSION

The term "definitive depression" deserves further consideration. It originates with the author, and its use is idiosyncratic to him. Nevertheless, he considers it to be of value in the presentation of the material at hand.

Definitive means fully developed or differentiated. The term implies that the major depressions have certain core elements in common, elements which are always present even though they may be overshadowed by striking differences between individual depressed patients. After all, depressions do not occur *in vacuo*. They occur as reactions to object loss (as we shall see later) in individuals with established adaptive, defensive, or regressive patterns or pathways. The fact that object loss occurs at different points in the life cycle and in individuals with different personality structures accounts for much of the variation in the clinical picture.

The term "definitive depression" further calls attention to the fact that depressions which have progressed beyond a certain point of severity (this point may be variously defined as loss of contact with reality, lack of response to supportive measures, or complete incapacitation) are relatively self-sustaining regardless of how the depression was initiated. Even restoration of the lost object, when this is possible, does not alleviate the depression.

THE PSYCHOLOGY OF DEPRESSION

A number of psychological theories have been proposed to explain depression. The most useful of these has been that which views depression as a *reaction to loss*. Depression is said to be the expression of both *grief* and *anger* in response to loss. This statement leads easily to the classic formulations of the dynamics of depression by Freud (3) and by Abraham (4). They saw depression as a regressive attempt at retaining the lost object by incorporating it into the self, while at the same time expressing rage against it for the desertion; and so rage is expressed against that part of the self which represents the introjected lost object. A number of alternative theoretical formulations exist, representing for the most part variations of this theme. The reader is referred to Myer Mendelson's excellent review of the subject for a fuller discussion than can be presented here (5). For our purposes, the less technical formulation will suffice: *Depression is a pathological reaction to object loss.*

What is meant by the phrase "pathological reaction to object loss?" All persons react to significant losses, usually with grief, and sometimes with anger. We consider such reactions to be pathological when they are out of proportion to the loss sustained, when they last too long, or when they are so severe as to incapacitate the individual.

Freud realized that a relation existed between normal grief and profound depression (melancholia). He expressed this relation as follows: "In grief it is the world which becomes poor and empty; in melancholia it is the ego itself." (3)

The Subjective Experience of Depression

What is the subjective experience of the depressed patient? Most people have been mildly dejected at one time or another; but this does not constitute the same kind of experience as being profoundly depressed, day after day over weeks or months. The question, therefore, cannot be answered by introspection.

Next, we can go to the patient himself and ask him about his subjective experience. Our efforts in this direction are hampered by the fact that depressed patients are either unwilling or unable to say very much about their feelings; their thought processes are slowed; and the interest that attaches to outside stimuli is indeed small. When they do speak about their feelings they are apt to do so in a repetitive or stereotyped manner; and we do not learn a great deal from that. Thus, we are left relatively in the dark about the mental state of the patient who exclaims from time to time: "God help me, God help me." Then too, once the patient has made a recovery from his depression, he may either not remember how he felt (amnesia due to electroconvulsive therapy) or he may be unwilling to revive painful memories.

When the direct path to knowledge is blocked, indirect ways may be tried. One attempt at learning more about the subjective experience in depressed patients that has met with some success is the investigation of dreams (6). The depressed patient may be just as unwilling to tell his dreams as he is to tell anything else. But if he does so, what he says is likely to be rather revealing. The dream, in pictorial or metaphorical language, perhaps better than anything else, conveys something of the essence of feeling depressed. A few examples may be cited.

A married housewife in her late thirties, given to periodic mood swings, became profoundly depressed when her daughter became pregnant out of wedlock. She became delusional over her physical health and felt she would be dead within the year. Because of this she had given up a part-time job she had held for some years. She had the following dream: "I am back at work." This was all she told of the dream at first. But then she continued. "I am back at my job. I am trying to do the work, but I know I can't. I just can't. I feel terrible about it." Another depressed patient dreamed: "I am in a nursing home. I call for the nurse but when she comes I can't recognize her. When I look up again, she's gone. I know that no matter what happens to me, I am all alone, no one is there to help me." And another dream: "I am in a strange city. I am trying to find my way. I stop people to ask for directions; but they all turn away. I am tired; I have a long way to go; I've lost my way."

In such dreams we find the main theme of depression: *object loss*, whether the object be a loved person, a prized ability, a cherished dream, pride, honor, or money. Loss is the heart of the psychology of depression.

THE PHENOMENOLOGY OF DEPRESSION

The clinical picture of severely depressed patients varies a good deal. However, experience has taught us to look for a *core group of signs and symptoms* without which it would be difficult to establish the presence of depression in patients. The symptoms are as follows: abject and painful sadness; generalized withdrawal of interest and inhibition of activity; and a pervasive pessimism, manifesting itself as severely diminished self-esteem and a gloomy evaluation of one's future as well as one's present situation. When looked for, these symptoms may be found in nearly all severely depressed patients, although at times other, more dramatic, symptoms may be so much more in the foreground as to draw attention away from the basic symptoms. They are of particular significance if they represent a change from the patient's usual way of feeling, thinking, and behaving and if they persist, day after day, without relief.

There is a second group of pathological phenomena, more properly called *signs* than symptoms, which has a significance roughly comparable to the presence of the core psychological symptoms. These are the *biological signs* of depression. The term "biological sign" does not imply that these signs are biochemically caused, although future research may well prove them to be so caused. At our present state of knowledge, however, it merely alludes to the fact that the manifestations of severe depression are not confined to the psychological sphere alone; they affect the whole organism. The biological signs of depression are as follows: sleeplessness; loss of appetite; weight loss; constipation, or more rarely diarrhea; psychomotor retardation, or more rarely, psychomotor agitation; and daily repeated mood cycles, particularly those characterized by profound depression early in the day, with gradual lifting of the mood as the day wears on.

Grinker and his colleagues (7) have recently brought a fresh approach to the phenomenological study of depression. Using the technique of factor analysis, they have described a number of factors in depression, one or more of which may be present in any given patient. A factor is defined as a *cluster* of symptoms, all of which tend to be present if any one of them is present.

The factor which can be identified most reliably and which occurs in nearly all depressed patients is the basic depression factor, corresponding more or less to the basic symptoms outlined above. In addition, Grinker et al. have described a number of other factors, or constellations of symptoms, which may be present and which, by their presence, may significantly change the total picture.

One of the most frequent of these is that in which patients experience profound feelings of guilt over minor actual or major fantasied wrong-doing. These patients are preoccupied with future punishments or with attempts to make restitution. They may employ projective mechanisms which may lead to delusions and hallucinations. The content of these delusions, however, is understandable once the basic premise of profound wrong-doing is accepted. Put another way, the content of hallucinations and delusions in such patients is congruent with the prevailing affect. At times guilt and self-accusation have been included as part of the basic factor of major depressions, but neither Grinker nor the present author subscribes to this view. Delusional guilt is seen frequently but not universally in definitive depression.

Another cluster of symptoms which can be delineated in depression is that of severe anxiety. This may range from subjectively experienced tenseness to external signs of anxiety. These may include anything from tremulousness of the hands to total body agitation, with pacing, hand-wringing, clawing at bed clothes, and even attempts at self-mutilation.

A factor seen somewhat less frequently is that of marked somatic or hypochondriacal preoccupation. Such patients insist that there is something physically wrong. They may demand that something be done, be it further laboratory studies, repeated physical examinations, the giving of pills or of shock treatment. These patients are often demanding, whining, and clinging, evoking anger in physicians and nursing staff.

Still another, and fairly clearly distinguishable, constellation of symptoms is that of the patient maintaining, against all reason, that everything would be all right and he would no longer be depressed "if only" some single factor in his situation were changed. Such a patient may say that his problems would vanish "if only" he had a better job, if he had more education, if a lawsuit had gone another way.

Clinical pictures such as we have described can appear in pure culture or in combination. In addition, other kinds of symptoms which do not readily fit into a depressive pattern may be seen. Here we wish to call attention to those patients who respond to loss or the threat of loss primarily with an exacerbation of neurotic, or characterological, or somatic symptoms. For instance, hysterical women may, at the time of menopause or in response to the loss of a loved one, become more demanding, whining, and clinging. Their provocative characterological traits may dominate the picture, allowing the depression to go unidentified. Likewise, persons with rigid, obsessive character structures may react to loss with an increase in their obsessions or compulsions, at times to the point of total incapacitation. Often the basic symptoms of depression are also present and can be elicited if the examiner is not deceived by the presence of flagrant characterological symptoms.

We said earlier that much of the variation in the clinical picture of depressed patients can be accounted for on the basis of interaction between personality structure and the task of dealing with a perceived loss. The patterns of depressive symptomatology outlined above are reflections of such interactions. It is not possible to describe here in detail what kind of personality will respond in which way to what kind of stress or loss; nor is the relationship necessarily one to one. What is important here is that we look for meaning in the patient's symptomatology. Symptoms express something about the patient's situation, something he wants, or fears, or feels. We must ask ourselves: Why did this person react to this particular stress in this particular way, and at this time?

NOMENCLATURE

To the present author the usual separation of the major depressive reactions into psychotic depressive reactions, involutional psychotic reactions, and manic-depressive reactions is not warranted; he prefers to think of them as definitive depressions, or as major affective disorders, for the reasons indicated earlier. Such separation, however, continues to be made in the minds of many, and one needs to know on what basis this is usually done (8).

A first episode of major depression is usually labeled *psychotic depressive reaction*. A major depression occurring during the climacteric is usually identified as an *involutional psychotic reaction*, particularly when thought content revolves around loss of sexual function or generalized somatic concerns, or when paranoid ideas are prominent. When there is a history of previous depressions, when the first depression occurred well before age forty, when episodes of mania or hypomania have been identified, or when there is a history of personality pattern given to periodic mood swings (cyclothymic personality), then the diagnosis of *manic-depressive reaction* is made.

TREATMENT OF PATIENTS WITH MAJOR DEPRESSIVE DISORDERS

Psychotherapy

The use of psychotherapeutic techniques alone has been tried in the treatment of major depressions (9), but they have, unfortunately, several very serious limitations: profoundly depressed patients have great difficulty in engaging in an ongoing psychotherapeutic relationship, particularly one which depends on a continued dialogue between patient and therapist; results can be achieved only slowly, if at all, thus leaving the patient exposed to suffering and to suicidal risk for needlessly long periods; and since the psychotherapeutic process is a slow one, and since spontaneous remissions occur, it is difficult to tell whether improvement has occurred spontaneously or as a part of treatment. On the other hand, re-educational or conflict-solving psychotherapy during the symptom-free periods between depressions may be able to bring about basic changes in personality structure and thereby decrease the likelihood of future episodes of depression.

Electroconvulsive Therapy

Ewalt and Farnsworth state categorically (10): "Electroconvulsive therapy given about three times per week is the quickest and most effective method of terminating a severe episode of psychotic depression." We are in agreement with this view, and the clinical practice in many private and university hospitals is largely along these lines. Electroconvulsive therapy is an entirely empirical method for the treatment of major depression. It consists of a series (usually from 6–12) electrically induced grand mal seizures. These are usually administered in conjunction with a muscle relaxant (in order to minimize the possibility of bone fracture) and under short-term anesthesia (to allay anxiety and to prevent recall of the procedure). ECT is particularly indicated when continued active suicide impulses plague the patient (suicides can occur even in hospitals) or when agitation is so marked or food intake is so impaired that physical exhaustion or physiological imbalance (dehydration, starvation, cardiac failure) threatens.

ECT should never be the sole mode of therapy. It should always be supplemented by psychotherapeutic efforts before, during, and after the administration of ECT. These are used in two ways: to help the patient understand the treatment itself, and to help him cope with his depression.

The first task is to explain to the patient in a realistic way and in lay terms, the nature and purpose of electroconvulsive therapy; when and how it is to be given; and what subjective sensations he may expect, before, during, and after treatment. A temporary delirium, with some confusion and disorientation, regularly results from shock therapy after two or more treatments. The total reversibility of this needs to be explained to the patient, in fact, perhaps repeatedly so, since as the delirium increases the doctor's explanations may not be recalled from one day to the next. The relatives of the patient, too, need to be similarly informed. There is a small but definite risk associated with the administration of shock therapy, and the relatives at least, if not the patient himself, need to be apprised of this. In rare instances, bone fractures can occur and, more rarely still, cardiac complications arise. The risk of these is extremely small when compared with the risk of suicide or other self-damage in untreated cases.

The second area of supportive psychotherapeutic effort is in dealing with depression itself. As we have mentioned, patients in the depth of their depression are only minimally available for verbal interchange. Nonetheless, there are a number of psychological interventions that the physician can make which are meaningful to the patient. Surprisingly, a sympathizing approach to the patient's problems is nearly always ineffective, and not infrequently leads to an exaggeration of symptoms, particularly self-accusations, proclamations of guilt, and recitations of past sins and expected punishments. The patient will claim, and quite justly so, that the therapist has failed to understand him. On the other hand, the therapist can state, quite realistically, that he realizes that the patient is abjectly depressed; that he knows that the patient himself feels there is no hope for him or his miserable condition; that in his practice he has seen many patients with similar problems who did, after all, get better even though they had given up all hope. He can also say that this condition tends to be self-limiting and is subject to complete remission even without treatment, but remission can be speeded up by various therapeutic techniques. He may finally say that he realizes that the patient may derive no immediate benefit from such optimistic predictions but that in time he will come to know that the physician was correct in his appraisal of the situation. Patients at times hardly acknowledge such statements, or dispute them vigorously and aggressively with the therapist. Following the abatement of the depression, however, many patients tell the doctor that he did penetrate the barriers they had erected against hope, and that they clung to his words through the worst moments of their depression. The physician has this on his side: his benign predictions correspond to clinical fact. Nine out of ten times, or very close to that, patients with affective disturbances recover.

Drug Therapy

In recent years, beginning in 1957, a number of drugs have been introduced for the treatment of depression (11). They have raised the hope that chemotherapy might become an effective replacement for electroconvulsive therapy, and that, in addition, drugs might be used where ECT was either contraindicated or ineffective. The initial enthusiasm for these drugs has had to be tempered considerably. On the one hand, their efficacy seems to be of a lower order of magnitude than that of ECT and their range of usefulness narrower than had originally been believed. On the other hand, side effects have been frequent and troublesome, and a number of drugs have had to be withdrawn from the market. Nevertheless, these so-called antidepressant drugs do represent a valuable new treatment which is flexible, convenient, and reasonably effective. In addition, these drugs have given fresh impetus to research into the biochemical causes and/or concomitants of depression. The so-called catecholamine hypothesis of affective disorders (see below) is one outgrowth of such studies (12).

Chemically, the drugs in current use fall into two classes: monoamine oxidase inhibitors (principally Marplan, Nardil, Niamid, and Parnate) and anti-depressant drugs without monoamine oxidase inhibitor activity (principally Tofranil, Elavil, and Aventyl). It is felt that their basic mood-elevating effect is produced through the increase or potentiation of brain norepinephrine (and/or other centrally active catecholamines). This is accomplished in the case of the monoamine oxidase inhibitors by the decreased enzymatic breakdown of brain norepinephrine, in the case of Tofranil (chemically imipramine) by the inhibition of cellular uptake of norepinephrine in the brain, thus again increasing the effective level of brain norepinephrine. This theory does not explain whether changes in brain transmitter amines are causally or concomitantly related to clinical states of depression, but it does open up avenues for further study of these questions.

The one drug which has enjoyed the greatest favor and most extensive use among clinicians is Tofranil. Chemically it is related to the phenothiazines, but differs from it in its activity. When used in adequate dosages of 75 mgm to 300 mgm daily, it produces improvement in perhaps half the cases of deep (hospitalized) depression. Exact figures vary a great deal, ranging from improvement in nearly 90 per cent of cases to no greater improvement than that seen with placebo treatment. When Tofranil is used in the lesser depressive states and on an out-patient basis, its efficacy becomes much harder to evaluate. In general it is felt that Tofranil works best in cases in which ECT also works best. Onset of action takes from several days to several weeks, and maintenance therapy at lower doses is recommended after remission has occurred. The fact that onset of action is slow tends to complicate evaluation in a disorder which is characterized, after periods of time, by spontaneous remissions. Side effects of the drug are numerous, although for the most part not grave. Kalinowsky, for instance, lists no fewer than eighteen, including, among others, dry mouth, dizziness, hypotension, fatigue, tremors, and occasionally, delirious syndromes (11). Likewise, for the monoamine oxidase inhibitor drugs the same author lists no fewer than twelve possible complications.

Perhaps the best that can be said about the drug treatment of the depressions at this time is that we may be on the right track, both theoretically and clinically. In the meantime, thorough familiarity with all three treatments (psychotherapy, electroconvulsive therapy, and chemotherapy) is necessary.

SPECIAL FORMS OF DEFINITIVE DEPRESSION

We turn our attention next to several subtypes of depression whose features are sufficiently unique to deserve special consideration. These are the schizo-affective disorders and the depressions of the postpartum period.

Schizo-Affective Disorders

The official term for these disorders, according to the American Psychiatric Association nomenclature, is *schizophrenic reaction, schizo-affective type*. These patients are schizophrenic. In addition, they are depressed in a major way. The disorder is seen primarily in persons in their twenties and thirties. Onset of symptoms is usually rapid, and although precipitating circumstances may be identifiable these are not usually of sufficient gravity to explain in any realistic sense the magnitude of the reaction. These patients show schizophrenic thought disorder, with illogical, arbitrary, autistic, or bizarre thought processes. Depression is also present to an overwhelming degree, manifesting itself in bizarrely nihilistic delusions, refusal to have any human contact, delusional self-accusations, and sometimes profound psychomotor retardation. Anxiety is a regular accompaniment of the disorder, and is apt to be massive. In short, these patients are deeply depressed, but at the same time they are at the brink of total personality dissolution.

Schizo-affective reactions tend to respond well to short courses of electroconvulsive therapy (2 to 5 treatments). Dramatic improvement can often be seen after even one or two treatments, with simultaneous disappearance of depression, anxiety, and psychotic thought processes. Recovery is often seemingly complete. Follow-up of such patients, however, shows that they may have recurrences of similar or totally different schizophrenic syndromes in subsequent years. Even in those patients that have no clear-cut recurrence, some residual deficit can usually be found, such as blunting of affect, decrease in social contact, or occasional autistic or metaphorical thinking. In other words, there is residual schizophrenic defect (see next chapter).

Postpartum Psychosis

The term "postpartum psychosis" has been applied to psychiatric disorders which have their onset immediately following or within six months of parturition. *Some* emotional upheaval or instability is a common, almost a universal, experience for women two to five days after delivery. Euphoria may be experienced, but depression is by far the more common phenomenon. In lay language this is referred to as "the baby blues."

In some persons this rather common experience develops into

a full-blown psychotic illness. The frequency of psychotic reactions in the postpartum period is considerably greater than for a non-postpartum group of women of the same age. There are several possible reasons. One explanation involves the radical changes in endocrine balance which takes place two to five days after delivery, amounting to virtually complete withdrawal of previously very high levels of sex hormones. This fact has led some investigators to postulate an organic (biochemical) basis for these reactions. Adding support to this contention is the observation of confusional or delirium-like states in these reactions, and the occasional presence of abnormal EEG patterns. Another explanation concerns the radical change in the relationship between mother and child. The fetus, felt by the mother to be a part of her, has become an external object. Some would blame this (psychological) change for the resulting disturbance. Adding support to this contention is the fact that these women are primarily preoccupied with and disturbed by their feelings for and their relationship with the newborn child (13).

The term "postpartum psychosis" covers at least two major groups of clinical pictures, one in which depression predominates, the other in which schizophrenia-like symptoms occur. The schizophrenia-like picture most often resembles an acute undifferentiated schizophrenic reaction, and will not be discussed further at this point.

The depressive picture is characterized by sadness and loss of interest, particularly by loss of interest in the care of the child. Fatigue and insomnia are experienced and are blamed on the newborn. Suicidal impulses and homicidal impulses directed against the child may occur. At the same time patients experience guilt feelings over their neglect of and anger toward the child. Many such women feel inadequate as mothers and are unsure of their role in relation to the baby.

In a number of psychiatric treatment centers simultaneous hospitalization of mother and child in one hospital ward has been

carried out (14). The aim of this is to allow the patient to continue to function in her role as mother while receiving help with
her psychological problems.

Treatment of the postpartum psychoses may be by psychotherapy alone, with the focus on the mother's ambivalent feelings
toward her child. Or it may, in addition, involve the use of tranquilizers or of ECT. The phenothiazines (e.g. Thorazine) are
sometimes used to control massive anxiety or threatened loss of
impulse control. ECT may be used when depression is unremitting
or when suicidal risk is prominent.

The long-term prognosis for this group of disorders is uncertain.
Some have no further difficulty after their initial disturbance has
been resolved. Others have recurrences after the delivery of the
next child, while still others may show rather typical cyclical
affective disturbances, or even develop classical symptoms of
chronic schizophrenia.

MANIA OR ELATION

The terms "mania" and "elation" will be used interchangeably.
Mania occurs less frequently than depression and is perhaps
somewhat less well understood. It is a psychopathological reaction
pattern which has a very special relation to depression, on several
counts. First, it often precedes or follows major depressive reactions. Also, persons who have experienced either mania or depression at some time in their lives run a greater risk of experiencing
the opposite reaction pattern at some future time than does the
population at large. Third, its symptomatology in many, though
not in all, ways is an exact opposite or mirror image of what is
seen in depression. Kraepelin recognized this intimate relationship between manic and depressive reaction patterns in his term
"manic-depressive psychosis" (1). Finally, as further evidence of
this close relationship, we observe that the same kind of psychological crisis situation which at one time gives rise to a depressive

reaction, may at another time, or in another person, set off a manic reaction.

The Psychology of Mania

We stated earlier that depression, from a psychological point of view, represents a pathological reaction to object loss. Mania, too, represents a pathological reaction to object loss, with a difference. Mania is a more primitive, more maladaptive reaction pattern than is depression: it makes use of more primitive, more maladaptive defenses. This results in greater disruption of reality testing (the capacity to correctly perceive and interpret reality) and, in terms of the clinical picture, a more flagrant psychosis. In fact, manic patients epitomize mental illness to the layman. Historically, the term "mania" was used to stand not only for elation but for madness generally.

The principal defense mechanism employed in the manic reaction is *denial*. An object loss has occurred, but is perceived as so overwhelming or so intolerable to the ego that it cannot be accepted. Hence, the loss is *denied* (15). It may be useful to recall at this point that denial normally is the first reaction to significant object loss. The assassination of President Kennedy provided a dramatic instance of this. The news that he had been shot was received with a vehement "No!"—a denial; then a period of stunned shock followed, and finally painful grief. To the person destined to become manic, the insult or loss is so devastating that he cannot permit himself to acknowledge that it has occurred. Denial sets in. In order to keep from consciousness a loss of such great significance, denial cannot be selective; it must be broadly applied: not only did the loss not occur, but all other inadequacies, limitations, and frustrations do not exist. This broad denial of all things unpleasant results in the typically exuberant, ebullient, elated mental state which we know as mania. It is also responsible for that aspect of the reaction which makes mania an illness and a psychosis. When major portions of reality are denied, satisfactory adaptation to a realistic environment is no longer possible; sound and logical judgments can no longer be formed. Instead, affect, activity, and thought content are determined by stimuli of the moment.

We have presented one theory of the psychology of mania. There is a second theory related to it (16) which holds that mania represents a denial, not of object loss but of depression. This is an older view, one that preceded the more precise characterization of mania as a denial of loss. Adherents to this theory point out that depression can always be seen just under the surface of the manifestations of mania. And the observation is, of course, correct. Most manic patients experience moments and sometimes prolonged periods of depression. But when the pain of depression becomes too great, denial once more takes over, and within seconds the patient may be again expansive and exuberant. Some manic patients, gradually or suddenly, become depressed and then run the course of a typical definitive depression. For, to be sure, the manic is merely postponing the inevitable; sooner or later he must deal with the loss. Only in so far as the patient may gain other objects or other support as time goes on (e.g. through treatment), or as the loss is viewed as less significant, can he relinquish his maladaptive defenses (denial) and permit the loss to come into consciousness.

PHENOMENOLOGY OF MANIA

The diagnosis of mania, as of all psychiatric entities, is made on the basis of the presenting clinical picture. In no other clinical syndrome is this richer and more varied. Yet from the wealth of observable data a few central features can be abstracted which regularly characterize the manic patient. They are: a subjective sense of extreme well-being; a heightened interest in and intense engagement with the surroundings, with speeding up of thought processes, of speech production, and of motor behavior; a pervasive optimism, manifesting itself in tremendously increased self-esteem and in a rosy view of the world and of the future. Comparing these symptoms with the basic symptoms of severe depression we find that they represent disturbances in the same area of behavior as are seen in depression but that the disturbances in mania are in the opposite direction from those in depression. Most of the remaining behavioral deviations of the manic patient can be reduced to these central tendencies.

"Biological signs" are not so well developed in mania as they are in depression, with one exception: insomnia is regularly part of the clinical picture. Manic patients rarely sleep more than a few hours a night, and this not continuously. Weight loss, too, is observed, but this is due not so much to loss of appetite (as it is in depression) as to inattention to food intake and to increased energy expenditure.

Manic patients usually have no insight into their illness and hence do not seek psychiatric help for themselves. They are *brought* to the psychiatrist by relatives, friends, and sometimes by the police. A rather typical history may be obtained:

The patient is a middle-aged man who had been well until several months ago, when his closest friend and long-time business associate died unexpectedly of a heart attack. For a few weeks the patient was sad and dejected, but soon his behavior changed. He became increasingly more active in his business and a good deal more talkative. He made many phone calls, talked of new and highly lucrative business schemes, spoke of taking a trip, first to Hawaii, then to Hong Kong, or perhaps around the world. He wrote innumerable letters to travel agencies, banks, and resorts, as well as to important personages such as the governor and the President. His secretary noted that these letters were marked "Important" in large writing on the outside of the envelope. The man began to spend a great deal of money, not only for himself but also for casual acquaintances. In one week he bought a new sports car and a piece of property by the lake, neither of which could he afford. He talked loudly and constantly to everyone he met. His usual reserved manner and social inhibitions seemed to have disappeared. He slept little, smoked to excess, and drank more than had been his custom formerly. Generally he was in good cheer, but he quickly became irritated and sometimes intensely angry when he met with any kind of frustration. His family noted that he was easily distracted, that his conversation seemed to move swiftly from topic to topic without ever really getting anywhere. They noted that he liked to make jokes and puns, and seemed to be very fond of hearing his own voice. He rejected all concerns over his well-being with the statement that he felt "like a million bucks." Soon after that he called up a broker friend and ordered him to buy a million dollars' worth of stock in the Xerox Corporation. The broker, who was a close friend and knew his financial situation, demurred on the order but came over to see him. His friend and his family finally realized that he was emotionally disturbed, and they persuaded him to go to the hospital. After initially resisting and becoming very angry at this idea, he again became cheerful, thought it was a good idea, and invited everyone in the family to come along. The psychiatric resident who saw him in the emergency room made prompt arrangement for his admission to a closed psychiatric ward.

When he was seen in his hospital room by the psychiatrist he appeared bright-eyed, alert, and in good humor. His movements were quick and graceful, his speech was rapid, lilting, full of alliteration and occasional rhymes. He welcomed the psychiatrist warmly and asked to be called by his first name. He denied that anything was wrong, but offered suggestions on how the running of the hospital could be improved. When the doctor, in response to the patient's question, told him that he would not be allowed to leave the hospital, he became belligerent and seemed on the verge of hitting the psychiatrist. But he suddenly became interested in first the necktie, and later the fountain pen of the psychiatrist, saying: "That's a nice pen you got, Doc. We should become pen pals. I was in the pen once, for drinking. Come on, Doc, let's go out on the town and have a drink." Then he broke into song with "Drink to Me Only with Thine Eyes" and asked the psychiatrist to join in with him. When the doctor asked about the death of his friend, the patient became momentarily depressed. But he rallied quickly: "I've got a hundred friends. I've got a thousand friends, I've got more friends than anybody in the whole world. Ain't that right, Doc? You're my friend."

What has just been described is typical manic behavior in its outline, not in its details. The details vary endlessly from patient to patient, but they do not vary randomly or meaninglessly. They express, in disguised language, the major concerns and conflicts of the patient. In our example the patient's assertion that he had many friends, served as defense against the realization that he had been robbed by death of his closest friend.

MANAGEMENT OF THE MANIC PATIENT

The management of the manic patient must take into consideration that the patient is psychotic (17). His reality testing and his judgment are grossly defective. Left to his own devices, he will engage in excesses of every kind: financial, sexual, and alcoholic. These may result in irreparable damage to his financial or social position. His excessive physical activity may lead to exhaustion. Precipitous suicide is also a very real danger. Lacking internal controls to his behavior, the manic patient must be provided with external controls, and this can best be accomplished in the protective and limiting custody of a psychiatric hospital ward.

Often this measure alone is not enough. Safe in the confines of the hospital, his activity may continue at the same high pitch, or even spiral upwards. Further medical and psychological intervention is then necessary to avoid physiological exhaustion or further disorganization of psychological functioning. Close attention must be paid to maintaining adequate caloric and fluid intake. A thorough physical examination must be performed to detect any medical illness; for manic patients are unaware of, or unheeding of, pain or other warning signals. The psychological management consists in providing consistent and reasonable limits to the patient's activity, and in clarifying and defining his situation in structured and unambiguous terms. When these measures are insufficient, the addition of drug therapy is indicated. The phenothiazines (e.g. Thorazine), initially in large doses, are generally able to slow the excitement of manic patients to tolerable levels. ECT has also been tried but it is less consistently effective in terminating manic episodes than depressive episodes.

As the manic patient gradually becomes more calm, and as his attention span increases, he becomes able to engage in psychotherapeutic endeavors with the psychiatrist. The fact that he now can control his behavior and can relate to a physician who is interested in him results in an increase of self-esteem, now realistically based instead of being inflated through denial.

Management of the psychotherapeutic relationship with the manic patient is not easy. The patient often continues to be demanding and provocative. The psychiatrist must therefore guard against being manipulated by the patient and against becoming angry with him for his attempts at manipulation. He must also try to protect the patient from indulging in provocative behavior with other patients or staff which might lead to rejection and damage of self-esteem. In helping the patient deal with those factors which led to the manic reaction, he must be alert to the emergence of depression and, particularly, of suicidal impulses. He must guard against being manipulated into discharging the patient prematurely. For the goal of such manipulation may be the opportunity to commit suicide.

Manic episodes, like depressive episodes, tend to run their course and remit, if suicide can be prevented. However, patients who have had one manic episode are liable to recurrences, or to depressive episodes. Psychotherapy during the symptom-free period may decrease the likelihood of relapse. It can certainly be used to help the patient understand his propensity for deviant mood responses, and thus make him more willing to accept help should symptoms occur again.

HYPOMANIA

We have described mania in its fully developed form. But lesser forms of this same type of affective disturbance exist. These are referred to as *hypomania*. Hypomania may be episodic, just as mania is, but in a few persons this same type of reaction may go on for years so as to be regarded as part of the individual's character or personality. Hypomania is characterized by the same features as mania, but these are seen to a lesser degree. The hypomanic feels well, he is confident, sociable, and active. Hypomanic persons are often able to accomplish prodigious amounts of work during such phases. There is no clear-cut dividing line between mania and hypomania. Usually we call someone manic when his affective disturbance reaches a degree which significantly interferes with everyday functioning or when clear-cut breaks in reality testing occur.

MANIC SYMPTOMATOLOGY IN OTHER CLINICAL ENTITIES

Manic or hypomanic symptomatology may also be seen as part of other clinical syndromes, particularly schizophrenia and acute and chronic brain syndromes. When this is so the signs and symptoms of the basic disorder can be discovered alongside the manic symptomatology. For instance, patients with central nervous system syphilis may show expansive behavior, grandiose delusions, and elated affect; but the intellectual deficit can usually be elicited readily. The differentiation of mania from schizophrenia with an admixture of manic symptoms is somewhat more difficult. Schizophrenic grandiosity is apt to be more bizarre, and the association of ideas more private and less understandable. The association of ideas in manic excitement is determined primarily by external stimuli, while in the schizophrenic patient with manic features it is determined largely by inner stimuli. The psychology of manic symptomatology is presumed to be the same, wherever it occurs.

We have spoken here primarily of psychological theories of mania. In the light of present knowledge about the depressions, to which mania is intimately related, it would seem reasonable to suppose that future investigations of mania will reveal, in addition to the known psychological aberrations, biochemical aberrations which may be either causally or concomitantly related to it. At such a time the insights gained from a psychological approach to patients with excessive mood fluctuations will continue to be valuable.

REFERENCES

1. E. Kraepelin, *Manic-Depressive Insanity and Paranoia*, translated by E. Barclay, E. and S. Livingstone, Edinburgh, 1921.
2. Eugen Bleuler, *Dementia Praecox or the Group of Schizophenias*, International Universities Press, New York, 1950.
3. Sigmund Freud, "Mourning and Melancholia," in *Collected Papers IV*, Basic Books, Inc., New York, 1959.
4. Karl Abraham, "Notes on the Psychoanalytic Investigation and Treatment of Manic-Depressive Insanity and Allied Conditions," in *Selected Papers on Psychoanalysis*, The Hogarth Press and the Institute of Psychoanalysis, London, 1911.
5. Meyer Mendelson, *Psychoanalytic Concepts of Depression*, Charles C. Thomas, Springfield, Ill., 1960.
6. Aaron T. Beck and Clyde H. Ward, "Dreams of Depressed Patients," *Arch. Gen. Psychiat.*, 5:462–7, 1961.
7. Roy Grinker, Sr., *et al.*, *Phenomena of Depression*, Introductory Chapter only, Hoeber, New York, 1961.
8. Committee on Nomenclature and Statistics of the American Psychiatric Association. *Diagnostic and Statistical Manual*, American Psychiatric Association, Washington, D.C., 1952.
9. Mabel Blake Cohen, *et al.*, "An Intensive Study of Twelve Cases of Manic-Depressive Psychosis," *Psychiatry*, 17:103, 1954.
10. Jack R. Ewalt and Dana L. Farnsworth, *Textbook of Psychiatry*, McGraw-Hill Book Co., New York, 1963.
11. Lothar B. Kalinowsky and Paul H. Hoch, *Somatic Treatments in Psychiatry*, Grune & Stratton, New York, 1961.
12. Joseph J. Schildkraut, "The Catecholamine Hypothesis of Affective Disorders: A Review of Supporting Evidence," *Amer. J. Psychiat.*, 122:509–22, 1965.
13. James Alexander Hamilton, *Postpartum Psychiatric Problems*, Mosby, St. Louis, 1962.
14. H. Grunebaum and J. L. Weiss, "Psychotic Mothers and Their Children: Joint Admission to Adult Psychiatric Hospital," *Amer. J. Psychiat.*, 119:927–33, 1963.
15. B. Lewin, "Some Psychoanalytic Ideas Applied to Elation and Depression," *Amer. J. Psychiat.*, 116:38, 1959.
16. B. Lewin, *The Psychoanalysis of Elation*, Norton, New York, 1950.
17. Joseph Lichtenberg, "Theoretical and Practical Considerations of the Management of the Manic Phase of Manic-Depressive Psychosis," *J. Nerv. Ment. Dis.*, 129:243, 1959.

3

Schizophrenia

"It flays the mind but leaves the body whole."

INTRODUCTION

Schizophrenia is still psychiatry's major unsolved clinical and theoretical problem. Schizophrenic patients occupy more beds in mental hospitals than do patients with any other psychiatric disorder. The amount of money spent on the care of schizophrenic patients and the amount of productivity lost as a result of this illness can be measured in the billions of dollars in the United States alone; the suffering to which it leads, in patients and in their families, cannot be measured. Nevertheless, the causes of schizophrenia remain shrouded in mystery. To be sure, the *number of theories* has increased vastly since Bleuler first outlined this group of disorders in 1911 (1). Yet today even the general direction from which etiological answers will ultimately come cannot be agreed upon. Many investigators believe that the ultimate answers will come from the biological sciences (biochemistry, neurophysiology, genetics) and just as many that the social sciences (psychology, sociology, anthropology) will be the source. In the meantime the practising psychiatrist is confronted daily with new and old patients who "are" schizophrenic or who, in a very literal sense, *suffer from schizophrenia*. There can be no doubt that today such suffering can be relieved more often than

35

was possible only half a century ago. And the psychiatrist can often understand, at least in part, why a particular individual fell ill at a particular time in a particular way. It is felt that the doctor's ability to understand his patient's symptoms has a great deal to do with his ability to help that patient (2, 29).

The symptomatology of schizophrenia is exceedingly varied. It has taken monumental efforts on the part of many investigators, working together and alone, in concert or in opposition, to bring some order to this confusing and bewildering picture. But over the past seventy-five years we have begun to understand at least some portion of the seemingly senseless productions and actions of schizophrenic patients.

Which of the multiplicity of features of schizophrenia is to be regarded as essential or primary? While no one feature of schizophrenia qualifies for the designation of chief defect, several are mentioned with sufficient frequency and with sufficiently convincing supporting evidence to be regarded as the identifying characteristics of this group of disorders. They are as follows: one, a specific type of thinking disturbance, variously described as "loosening of associations," "dissociation," or "cognitive slipping"; two, defective development of the self-concept and of ego boundaries, i.e. decreased ability to distinguish self from others, and decreased ability to distinguish stimuli arising within the self from those arising in the outside world; three, a basic inability to form meaningful relationships with other people; four, a defect in the integrating and organizing functions of the personality (3–8).

It is thought that other features of schizophrenia, such as delusions, hallucinations, social withdrawal, and so forth, are adaptive or defensive mechanisms, employed to deal with one or more of the basic deficiencies outlined above. It must be made clear that the considerations presented here are phenomenological, not etiological, considerations. The difficult question of etiology will be discussed below.

Development of the Concept of Schizophrenia

Many great names in psychiatry are associated with the evolving concept of schizophrenia. In fact, few psychiatrists have attained stature without making some major contribution to our understanding of schizophrenia. Around the turn of the century Kraepelin classified as dementia praecox a group of diverse clinical entities previously thought to bear no relationship to one another: paranoia, catatonia, and hebephrenia (9). The common elements in these disorders, as he saw them, were onset at an early age and a progressively deteriorating course. But these were not the only features they had in common, for long after the idea of progressive deterioration proved untenable, the three entities continued to be associated with each other and today still form the central core among the subtypes of schizophrenia.

Bleuler, a Swiss psychiatrist, though disputing the uniformly poor prognosis postulated by Kraepelin, nonetheless recognized Kraepelin's grouping as sound. In a work which stands at the acme of phenomenological studies in clinical psychiatry (1911), he stated that there was indeed a group of psychiatric disorders, more or less identical with Kraepelin's dementia praecox cases, but which he preferred to call the *group of schizophrenias*. He described four fundamental symptoms characteristic of these disorders: disturbances of association; disturbance of affect; extreme ambivalence; and autism. These came to be known as the 4 A's of Bleuler. He also contributed one of the more concise definitions of schizophrenia.

By the term "dementia praecox" or "schizophrenia" we designate *a group of psychoses* whose course is at times chronic, at times marked by intermittent attacks, and which can stop or retrograde at any stage, but does not permit a full *restitutio ad integrum*. The disease is characterized by a specific type of alteration of thinking, feeling, and relation to the external world which appears nowhere else in this particular fashion (1).

Between 1906 and 1910 in the United States Adolf Meyer was developing the first truly dynamic concept of schizophrenia (17). Rather than looking at schizophrenia as an illness which somehow befell individuals, he saw it as a total *psychobiological reaction pattern* to life circumstances, under which rubric he included physical make-up as well as individual experiences. In language at times inarticulate he made the point that mind and body had for too long been treated as separate entities. He could nowhere discover a cleavage plane between body and mind. His holistic approach to patients as organismic entities rather than as conglomerates of bodily and psychic systems has profoundly influenced American psychiatry in its approach not only to schizophrenia but to other disorders as well.

Freud's contribution to the study of schizophrenia was less specific than that of Bleuler; perhaps it has had a more fundamental leavening effect. He suspected, and later demonstrated lucidly and convincingly, that mental processes and mental products were not random, or meaningless, or beyond understanding. Although his work, with the exception of the study of the diary of one schizophrenic patient, the Schreber Case (10), concerned itself primarily with the meaning of mental products of normal persons (dreams, slips of the tongue) and of neurotic patients (hysterical or obsessive symptoms), others have applied his principles to the study of the language and thought of schizophrenic patients. Beyond looking for meaning in the symptoms of schizophrenic patients, Freud's delineation of the types of thinking processes, the primary process (pleasure-oriented) and secondary process (reality-oriented) laid the foundation for studying the form as well as the content of schizophrenic language productions. His study of defense mechanisms, particularly of projection, denial, and repression, has found ample application in the study of schizophrenia. At no time in his life, however, did Freud focus on schizophrenia as a concept, nor did he ever knowingly attempt to treat schizophrenic patients (some of the patients he called neurotic would be classed as schizophrenic according to present criteria). Freud considered schizophrenia a "narcissistic neurosis," a term which implied, among other things, that such patients were unable to form the kind of positive attachment to a therapist necessary to carry out psychological treatment successfully. Other psychiatrists have rejected this notion of Freud's, at least in part, and perhaps chief of these has been Harry Stack Sullivan.

The contribution of Sullivan to the understanding of schizophrenia is actually difficult to summarize. He brought to it a complex, intuitive approach. But if his style of presentation was complex, so was the subject he was studying. He was convinced that schizophrenic patients *could be understood,* at least in part; at the same time he pointed to those aspects of schizophrenic symptomatology which by their nature could not be fully understood in logical verbal terms, i.e. in secondary process terms. Nevertheless he deplored the participation of the therapist in the patient's primary process productions. Sullivan was one of the first persons in this country seriously to espouse the psychotherapy of chronically schizophrenic patients; this, in fact, became his major life work. Through his experience with chronic schizophrenic patients, he found out that psychotherapy with such patients was feasible, but that rules which were applicable to the treatment of the neuroses either had to be abandoned or greatly modified, and that entirely new rules had to be developed. He believed that schizophrenia was a disorder characterized by difficulty in interpersonal relationships, from early days on. Working on this premise, he attempted to keep the interpersonal treatment situation as free from anxiety and as unambiguous as he knew how. He had some success in this, and many failures. He never spoke of cure, only of modification of the disorder (6).

Following Sullivan's lead, and to some extent independently, a number of other psychiatrists have taken up the challenge of attempting to treat this formidable disorder with psychological techniques. It is interesting to notice that many of these endeavors had their start in the Baltimore-Washington, D.C., area, where Adolf Meyer and Harry Stack Sullivan had worked, and that many others took their inspiration from the work of these two men.

Schizophrenic Thought Disorder

All who have studied schizophrenia have had this to say in common: Something is wrong with the schizophrenic person's mode of thinking. Bleuler described it as a peculiar "loosening of associations." Freud characterized it by comparing it with the processes of thought that occur with regularity in the dreamer, that is, the primary process. Sullivan referred to the schizophrenic's peculiar mode of thinking as being "related to modes of thinking which are proper to earlier phases of life and in which there is a predominance of nonverbal concepts," and in which there is an "extravasation of meanings beyond the specific things implied," and in which there is still great uncertainty about the boundaries between the self and the outside world. Kurt Goldstein felt that he could detect failure of abstraction in the thinking processes of schizophrenic patients, while Van Domarus, a logician, philosopher, and psychiatrist thought he could detect a law of logic which applied specifically to the thought process of schizophrenic patients. This has become known as *Van Domarus' Principle* or the *law of predicate logic:* two things are identical because they have one (important or unimportant) characteristic in common (4, 5). Example: patient to physician, "I know you are my father."—"Why do you say that?"—"Because my father had blue eyes." At that moment the schizophrenic patient is experiencing the physician *as* his father, not merely *like* his father. The experience is no doubt profoundly moving and perplexing to him (4, 5).

Meehl, in a recent attempt to come to grips with the problem of the peculiarities of schizophrenic thought processes, called this peculiarity "cognitive slipping," that is, a sometimes subtle derailment of thinking away from logical or goal-directed thinking, which is of the nature of an intellectual impairment but which doubtlessly results in profoundly moving emotional misunderstandings and painful social distance (3).

Psychiatrists have tried to view the peculiar mode of thinking which the schizophrenic patient shows as a deviation away from the norm rather than as something entirely new and in no way related to the experiences of normal persons. This has led a number of investigators to describe these thought processes or modes of thinking as a *regression* to the primary process mode of thought, thereby implying that the patient *has gone back* to using modes of thought which were once part of his normal development. But it must be pointed out that the term "regression" is in no way an explanation (i.e. a causal explanation) but rather a description of a mental mechanism. There is of course never complete regression, say, to the level of a three-year-old child. The regressed adult patient still has available to him adult modes of thinking, as well as a vast backlog of adult experience, which the child does not. In other words, he may use modes of thinking akin to those used by very young children, but he does not thereby become child-like in every way.

DEFENSE MECHANISMS IN SCHIZOPHRENIA

Defense mechanisms, or security operations, as Sullivan called them (11), are employed by all individuals, healthy or disturbed. The specific type of mechanism employed depends on the nature of the individual's internal or external conflicts as well as on the seriousness of the threat that such conflicts present. Reasonably healthy individuals may use defensive operations, such as repression, rationalization, identification with the aggressor, suppression, etc., from time to time and *flexibly*, as the need arises, without being limited in their over-all functioning by the automatic operation of these mental operations, and without sacrificing flexibility of adjustment in new situations. We consider the use of defensive operations as neurotic when it occurs *inflexibly* in given conflict situations and when it leads to symptom formation. In general we like to think of neurotic use of defensive mechanisms as being of such an order of magnitude that it produces only focal disturbance in an individual's functioning and causes no disturbance in an individual's functioning or reality testing.

In schizophrenia, which perhaps may be used as a model of the psychoses in general, the more highly differentiated and focused security operations are abandoned (in the face of massive threat of total personality disintegration) in favor of poorly differentiated, more primitive, and more maladaptive security operations —i.e. they are *emergency measures* in the face of severe threat.

We have already mentioned the frequent use of *regression* in schizophrenia. Regression tends to be general or global and takes in all or most areas of functioning. *Projection* is another frequently employed defense mechanism which stems from the very earliest years of life. It represents a protective spitting out of that which is unpalatable. The threat of internal dissolution or explosiveness is projected onto the outside world, often as world-wide destruction—e.g. a delusion develops that the world has been destroyed by nuclear holocaust. Similarly, self-accusatory judgments within the individual are projected onto the outside world—e.g. hallucinated voices are telling the disturbed individual that he is no good, that he is a freak, that he is a queer.

Denial also may be used frequently by schizophrenic patients. It, too, is a primitive mechanism and interferes with reality testing. A perception of moral worthlessness may be translated into its opposite—the patient says he is a prophet of God, or the Virgin Mary. Consensual validation and reality testing are lost.

Even more encompassing and more maladaptive still is *withdrawal*. Withdrawal is invoked when the threatening stimulus is either very great or when it is present for a prolonged period of time. The patient must protect himself from interactions with the world since all such interactions are experienced as painful by him. Such severe withdrawal from interaction may be seen in hebephrenic schizophrenic patients and in a certain percentage of chronically hospitalized schizophrenic patients. Catatonic stupor is probably a variant of this form of security operation, but is differentiated by its acute onset. Chronic withdrawal from interpersonal interaction probably is responsible for a large part of what is called intellectual and habit deterioration of schizophrenia.

It should be emphasized that any or all of these mechanisms may be employed in schizophrenia. Their presence alone, however, is not sufficient to warrant a diagnosis of schizophrenia. For instance, these same mechanisms may be employed in the psychotic reactions seen in organic brain deficit states.

ETIOLOGY OF SCHIZOPHRENIA

Kraepelin (9) felt that dementia praecox (schizophrenia) was caused by organic brain pathology; and although no specific brain pathology had been demonstrated (to date this is still true), he was convinced that it did exist, and with a refinement in technique would eventually be demonstrated.

Bleuler's views (1) on etiology were somewhat more modern. He too felt that the basic disturbance was an organic brain deficit, perhaps caused by some kind of intoxication (auto-intoxication?), but at the same time he felt that the specific form of the symptoms of each individual patient was psychologically determined. He was particularly influenced in this direction by C. G. Jung, who worked under him and who in turn had been strongly influenced by the teachings of Freud.

Kallmann (12) and others have held that schizophrenia is a hereditary disorder, i.e. the disturbance is carried in the genes, hence it is organic. Staying with the organic point of view but moving forward in time, we come to the work of Smythies (13) and others (Gottlieb et al.) who have found some evidence to suggest that disordered catecholamine (particularly adrenaline) metabolism may be associated with or may be the cause of schizophenia (14, 15). Several points need to be made about these various theories. First, these workers, with the exception of Kraepelin and

Bleuler (who only had "convictions"), have considerable amount of evidence on their side.

Careful review, however, by Kety (15) of the biochemical evidence and by Jackson (16) of the hereditary evidence led to serious questioning of both the evidence and the inferences. As to the biological causation of schizophrenia, we can reach only a Scotch verdict—"not proven."

Psychological etiologies began to be postulated with Freud (10), who held that *paranoid* schizophrenia at least was based on conflict over latent passive homosexual wishes. Freud never tried to deal with the whole of the schizophrenia problem.

Meyer (17) felt that psychological events did indeed influence the development and course of schizophrenic reaction patterns, but that biological givens were similarly important; he abhorred making this an either/or question.

Sullivan (6) put himself squarely on the psychological side of the question, holding that massive anxiety in the interpersonal area during childhood, latency, and adolescence had a causal connection with the development of schizophrenic symptomatology in early adult life.

Bateson and his group (18) in California and the Lidzs (19) at Yale have in recent years focused more sharply on the interaction between schizophrenic patients and their parents, particularly their mothers. They discovered that communication between these mothers and their children was grossly disturbed, particularly in the matter of contradictory (often mutually exclusive) parental expectations, thereby putting the child into a "double-bind" situation—you're damned if you do and damned if you don't.

One example of this kind of thinking and communication pattern (20) comes not from the clinical field but from a contemporary story: A mother gives her son two sport shirts for his birthday. The first time he wears one of them she looks at him and, with tears coming to her eyes, says: "You didn't like the other one?" Another example is this more authentic communication from a mother to her schizophrenic son (21):

Dearest Freddie,
  We heard your ring just as we were putting the key in the door—I am *so* thrilled—& wish you all the very best—Just get your school work & don't worry about anything else—Here is your chance, Honey & I know you will do well—You have what it takes—I'm very proud of you—Loads of love—Mother Moe is also happy for you & wishes you luck PPS If it doesn't work out—& you're not ready—don't worry—at least you tried.

A second brief excerpt from another letter will further illustrate the typical no-only-yes, do-yet-don't communication.

And don't you let the cigarette habit get stronger than you are. Sometimes these habits have a way of doing that. When I get a chance I'll get you a Carton.

Despite the cogency of these observations of disturbed mother-child communication, several important questions still go unanswered. One of these focuses on the specificity of this type of communication to the development of schizophrenia. Family interactions similar to those described for schizophrenic patients have been described for patients with psychosomatic disorders, particularly ulcerative colitis, and for psychopathic (sociopathic) conditions. Second, these observations do not explain why one child in a given family may develop schizophrenic reaction patterns while others either escape altogether or show only minor deviations from the norm. To the question of psychological etiology, too, we must offer a Scotch verdict—"not proven."

Many practising psychiatrists feel that both biological and psychological factors are important in the causation and development of schizophrenia. This is seen particularly in the area of modes of treatment, where even those who hold that schizophrenia is a hereditary affliction do not feel that psychological intervention is useless. Similarly, those convinced that schizophrenia is a purely psychological reaction pattern do not hesitate to use somatic therapies (especially Thorazine) for the control of acute and chronic symptomatology.

SCHIZOPHRENIC REACTION TYPES

When schizophrenic patients are observed over a long period of time it becomes apparent that a certain portion of them may at one point in time be dominantly catatonic but months or years later appear hebephrenic or paranoid; while another portion may no longer be ill at all or may retain a relatively unchanging constellation of symptoms. When one examines a population of schizophrenic patients at any single point in time, however, a number of types can be distinguished.

Schizophrenia, Acute Undifferentiated Type

Although the onset of schizophrenia is insidious in many patients, in many other persons the onset is fairly abrupt. When this is the case, patients may manifest some of the most grossly psychotic behavior and at this point correspond most closely to the layman's image of a "crazy" person. The most striking feature about such patients is the disturbance in every area of behavior—thinking, feeling, and acting. The outstanding affect is anxiety, sometimes approaching sheer panic. Attempting to convey an idea of the intensity of this anxiety, some psychiatrists have referred to it as "mega-anxiety." Accompanying this intense affect there is a gross disordering of thought processes; ideas expressed do not seem to follow logically (dissociation); the flow of ideas may be suddenly interrupted (blocking); new words are coined by the patient or else familiar words are combined into new words that have private meaning to the patient (neologisms, condensation, autism). At this stage the patient often has hallucinations (auditory hallucinations are most characteristic of schizophrenic patients) and expresses (often rapidly shifting) paranoid delusions. The patient usually is perplexed and bewildered, he may feel cornered or attacked, and may consequently wish to flee, or to attack, his supposed attackers. Many patients express religious ideas or frankly sexual ones, and the commingling of the two is not infrequent in schizophrenic patients. Lastly, many patients are uncertain as to their own identity and the identity of others; they may say that they feel they are about to explode, or that the universe is about to come to an end. Their ideas are often expressed under great pressure of speech, or else only haltingly, with many seemingly inexplicable interruptions. The anxiety of such patients is often so intense that even experienced psychiatrists are apt to become somewhat anxious vis-à-vis such patients.

Patients usually do not remain in this state for long, at least not with present methods of therapy. Gradually the anxiety decreases and other, more stable defenses begin to take over. Clearly the acute undifferentiated form of schizophrenia is only a phase from which a patient may either go on to recover or to develop other, more chronic forms of this disorder.

Schizophrenia, Hebephrenic Type

We may begin by saying that schizophrenic persons, like others, have a desire to communicate with others, and that this desire is a strong motivating force for much of the interaction, certainly most of the verbal or language interaction, that goes on between a person and those around him. As far as one can tell, hebephrenic patients no longer have this desire; they have written off any hope of ever making themselves understood. Though this statement is at best at the level of assumption, it can help us to understand somewhat better the puzzling clinical picture of hebephrenia. It is of hebephrenic patients that one can say with more justification than in any other instance that they "live in a world of their own." Meaningful communication has almost entirely disappeared, and what verbal productions one encounters, consisting of monosyllables, neologisms, ordinary words used with private meanings, or word salad, do not serve any recognizable purpose. Lacking a workable means of interacting with other persons, the patient shows rapid deterioration of habits, being inattentive to cleanliness or clothes. Interest in or performance of any purposeful activity disappears or is replaced by mannerisms or stereotyped behavior of doubtful symbolic meaning. The affective life is also altered. Frequently there is only a very narrow range of affect, interspersed with occasional smiling, giggling, or outright laughter. This so-called "silly" laughter gave the syndrome its name, but apart from the suggestion that such patients may be responding to pleasant hallucinations, very little is understood about "silly" laughter. This is not surprising, for hebephrenic patients who become dilapidated to this degree seldom recover, and while un-recovered are not able to shed much light on this question. Hebephrenic symptomatology has probably the worst prognosis of any of the constellation of symptoms. It usually occurs in patients who develop schizophrenic symptomatology at a young age (adolescence or pre-adolescence), and it represents probably the least successful adaptation to the basic schizophrenic defect.

Schizophrenia, Catatonic Type

The outstanding feature of the catatonic type of schizophrenic reaction is a dramatic change in motor activity, either in the direction of massive motor discharge (catatonic excitement) or in the direction of intense and active inhibition of virtually all motor activity (catatonic stupor). The two phases of catatonia may alternate rapidly with one another, or features of both excitement and inhibition may co-exist. In catatonic stupor there may be inhibition of not only the gross skeletal musculature but also of speech, swallowing, bladder, and rectum as well. Underlying the catatonic symptomatology is always a fantastically intense emotional turmoil, the presence of which can only be surmised by observing the catatonic patient when he is stuporous or mute.

However, it may become patently manifest in the often sudden, lightning-like discharges of verbal or physical assaultiveness (catatonic excitement). The catatonic state, rarely a stable condition, usually sets in after other schizophrenic symptoms, such as those described as being characteristic of the acute phase of the disorder, have been present for a shorter or longer period of time. Catatonic stupor may come about after a period of gradual slowing of activity, or it may set in either at a point of increasing anxiety or immediately after a burst of excited or destructive behavior.

Schizophrenia, Paranoid Type

It is perhaps a good time to define briefly what is meant by the paranoid attitude. Roughly, it is the attribution of malevolent intentions to persons or things in one's environment. It involves an extremely keen perception of any degree of hostility in the environment as well as the projection of the individual's own hostile or otherwise unacceptable intentions onto the outside world. A third factor is involved, an attitude which will be referred to as "causal scanning" of the environment. The schizophrenic patient perceives the world around him in a disordered way, and hence is always scanning the environment, trying to make connections, i.e. causal connections between events which may in fact have only a coincidental relation to one another. Another way of putting this is to say that the paranoid patient is very adept at theory-building on the basis of very flimsy evidence. Having defined paranoia in this way, we will go on to say that paranoid attitudes can be discovered in all or very nearly all schizophrenic patients at some point during their illness. In some patients, however, paranoid symptoms predominate or even become the only type of symptom. Early in the course of schizophrenia, paranoid delusions are apt to be rather inconstant, fluctuating from moment to moment; and they are associated with a great deal of anxiety. This state does not persist for long in most instances. The paranoid delusions either disappear or become fixed delusional systems, and concomitant with this development there is usually a marked decrease in anxiety. When this occurs, patients become less approachable from a therapeutic point of view. Many such patients, however, are then able to function fairly well in the community, although they may be troublesome to a great many people through their suspicious and frequently litigious attitude. Many patients who develop a fixed delusional system remain somewhat better integrated in the rest of their personality than do hebephrenic or chronic undifferentiated schizophrenic patients (see below). At times of stress, however, anxiety may recur, the delusional system may become much more highly charged emotionally, hallucinations may recur at this point or become more insistent, and such patients may then be driven to impulsive acts, either on the basis of delusional formulations or on the "instructions" of hallucinated voices. Classical psychoanalytical formulation holds that paranoia is a manifestation of conflict over latent passive homosexual wishes, presumably in all instances. While the question of homosexuality is a frequent concern in the productions of schizophrenic patients, it seems to constitute only a small part of the broader question of basic identity, i.e. whether the patient is man or woman, human or animal, dead or alive, self or other. As we have mentioned, this question of the adequate definition of ego boundaries is held by many to be one of the primary problems in schizophrenia.

Schizophrenia, Chronic Undifferentiated Type

Chronic undifferentiated schizophrenia is somewhat of a wastebasket term. It has only two meanings: that the schizophrenic symptomatology has been present for a long time; and that no *one* pattern of schizophrenic symptomatology sufficiently predominates to warrant a label such as hebephrenic, catatonic, or paranoid schizophrenia. Certainly some paranoid elements will be discovered in all schizophrenic patients who are still recognizably

ill. Patients described as showing chronic undifferentiated schizophrenia are often very lonely persons, leading restricted lives, with
a restricted range of affective experience. Subtle thought disorder
is often present which gives their verbal productions a somewhat
odd ring; words are used with somewhat idiosyncratic meanings.
Many such patients have delusional ideas or hear voices from time
to time, but except at times of increasing interpersonal stress,
these need not necessarily interfere greatly with their daily lives.
In a protected and rather isolated environment such persons can
hold jobs that are fairly mechanical or that bring them into fleeting and non-intense contact with others. Many such patients find
employment as park attendants, mail clerks, or as cashiers in
grocery stores or laundries. In any case, the level of job performance is generally well below that for which their original intellectual potential would have qualified them.

Schizophrenia, Pseudo-Neurotic Type

The pseudo-neurotic type of schizophrenia is one about which
there has been a good deal of disagreement: whether it exists as
a separate entity, whether it is in fact a schizophrenic disorder, and
how it might possibly be related to other forms of schizophrenia.
As it is commonly used, the term denotes those patients who have
been chronically plagued by a plethora of neurotic symptoms,
including phobias, obsessions, compulsions, doubting, and free-
floating anxiety (22). Sometimes this constellation of symptoms
is referred to as pan-neurosis. Such patients do not show any clear-
cut "thought disorder" of the type we have described earlier, nor
do they show schizophrenic responses on projective psychological
tests. Their neurotic symptomatology, however, does not respond
to intensive psychotherapy; in fact, their symptoms may become
worse or a frankly schizophrenic psychosis may emerge. Follow-up
of such patients over a number of years shows that a portion of
them will develop clear-cut schizophrenic psychoses at some point,
while others will persist in their pan-neurotic symptomatology

without much change. Spontaneous recovery is fairly rare (23).

Schizophrenia, Schizo-Affective Type

The schizo-affective type of schizophrenic reaction has been considered in Chapter 2, Affective Disorders.

TREATMENT IN SCHIZOPHRENIA

For many years the treatment of schizophrenic patients consisted of making the right diagnosis and in admitting such patients to mental institutions, where they received what amounted to little more than custodial care. In other words, the treatment of schizophrenic patients consisted of extrusion from the community and sequestration in "insane asylums" or "lunatic asylums." In these asylums, whether public or private, some patients lost their psychotic symptoms and were discharged as "spontaneous remissions." Another group improved in the hospital, but attempts to discharge them resulted in renewed psychotic symptomatology; such patients were relatively well as long as they remained in the confines of the hospital, but decompensated when faced with the stresses of "real life." Another large number of patients either did not improve at all or else changed for the worse: in the parlance of that day they "deteriorated" and became the "back-ward schizophrenics"—dilapidated, bizarre, out of contact with reality, with personality disintegration more or less complete.

But the treatment of patients with schizophrenic symptomatology has changed. Today treatment is *active*. Psychiatrists no longer stand by and watch "the disease unfold" or "the patient deteriorate," * although it sometimes happens that patients get worse or at least no better while active attempts at treatment are

---

* Today we are inclined to view "deterioration" not so much as an integral aspect of the progress of schizophrenia but as a result of chronic hospitalization per se (24).

being carried out. As long as the basic etiology of schizophrenic reaction patterns remains unknown, there can be no real "treating" of schizophrenia. At the human level, schizophrenia is or results in psychic suffering, and it is toward the amelioration of this suffering that the efforts of psychiatrists are directed. This is another way of saying that the treatment of schizophrenic patients is the treatment of symptoms.

In one way the therapeutic approach to schizophrenic patients has not changed: it still begins with the diagnosis. But making a diagnosis, the process of evaluating mental symptomatology, can and should be therapeutic in itself. It involves, *inter alia*, obtaining a psychiatric history, that is, a life history. There are few experiences in human life that are as meaningful as the recounting of one's life history, in full detail, to an interested, friendly, non-critical person. The schizophrenic patient does not expect strangers to be interested, friendly, or non-critical—his experience has taught him otherwise. If this experience of giving a psychiatric history comes off as a relatively anxiety-free interaction, then the groundwork is laid for establishing a meaningful relationship which will form the basis for later relationship therapy, probably one of the most important ingredients in all forms of psychiatric treatment.

Individual Psychotherapy

The psychiatrist who wishes to treat schizophrenic patients psychotherapeutically must demonstrate a high degree of flexibility in his approach to patients. His approach will not only vary from patient to patient, but it will also vary in different phases of the illness with the same patient. We will state here, for purposes of simplification, that the therapeutic appoaches can be divided into two categories: One, supportive psychotherapy, which attempts to improve the patient's psychological adaptation by helping him deal with present difficulties; two, definitive psychotherapy or insight-oriented psychotherapy, which tries to improve the patient's psychological adaptedness by helping him discover the root causes of the illness. There is a broad overlap between the two categories, and with most schizophrenic patients a period of supportive therapy must precede definitive, insight-directed therapy. There is one difference, however: while therapy of the former type is not committed in any way to any one etiological theory, the latter type of therapy implicitly or explicitly assumes a psychological causation of schizophrenia.

Supportive Psychotherapy

The acutely disturbed, grossly disorganized patient should be admitted to a psychiatric hospital ward. Once admitted, attention should be directed to reintroducing meaning and structure into the confused world of the patient. This cannot be done by the psychiatrist alone, but requires the joint efforts of the physician, nursing and aide personnel, and at times of fellow patients as well (25). The patient should be told, in unambiguous language, that he is in a psychiatric hospital, that the people around him are trying to help him and understand him. Patients are often grossly anxious and they may be experiencing frightening auditory hallucinations. A statement to the effect that the patient is safe in the hospital is often helpful. Above all, an empathic understanding, if it indeed exists, should be communicated to the patient. Mere placation or outright lies (so-called white lies) merely confirm the patient's view that people are not to be trusted, which can damage not only present but future treatment efforts. During the early stages of treatment, efforts at clarification and structuring the relationships and surroundings may need to be repeated frequently. The rationale for these maneuvers is based on the patient's psychopathological situation. To the acutely disturbed schizophrenic individual, the boundaries between self and others are not clearly delineated. He is involved in a spiraling problem: severe anxiety tends to erase ego boundaries, and inability to maintain ego boundaries increases anxiety. The psychiatrist will try to establish clearly defined ego boundaries and to keep them defined; he will also try to keep separate for the patient facts and fantasies. In so far as the patient has abandoned these important ego functions, the psychiatrist will assume them, temporarily, for the patient. At this point, anxiety-alleviating drugs (see below) may also be used to help the patient.

An acutely disturbed schizophrenic patient is often not able to tolerate any prolonged encounter with the psychiatrist at first. Patients communicate in a subtle or direct way, usually by a marked increase in anxiety, that they have reached the limit of their tolerance. On the other hand, frequent short visits with the patient are generally well tolerated and help to establish the relationship. Nowhere else is structure more important than in the communication about the psychiatrist's comings and goings. The patient needs to be told that the doctor is leaving, that he is coming back to see the patient, and when he is coming back to see the patient. A statement such as, "Well, I'll be leaving for now," does not suffice. A better statement would be, "I will be leaving now. I will be back to see you tomorrow morning at 8:00 a.m." If there is a change in the psychiatrist's schedule, the patient should be notified as soon as it becomes known to the doctor. Schizophrenic patients tolerate broken appointments poorly; to help them become oriented in what is, to them, a confusing world, the psychiatrist must try to present a clear and constant image.

Once a certain amount of reorganization of personality has been achieved the patient may ask: What happened? Patient and therapist alike are often puzzled about the events in the patient's life which preceded or led to psychotic breakdown. To make the sequence of events leading up to psychosis *understandable* is not merely an intellectual exercise but an important step in therapy. If doctor and patient can see that the psychotic reaction *makes sense*, that it is in some way understandable, then the patient can once more see himself as "much more simply human than otherwise."

Frequently, "what happened" can be discovered only by stages;

at first only general, perhaps metaphorical, answers can be supplied; later, specific events and their specific meaning to the patient may be elicited. This process of discovery is important, as we have said, in order to provide the patient with a sense of closure about the events. Also it is important to discover what specific type of interpersonal situation was disturbing to the patient in order that therapy may be directed either toward altering that particular pattern of behavior or else avoiding similar situations in the future. At this stage, insightful and supportive therapy may be intermingled and may enhance each other. The process of discovering the proximate causes of the psychotic breakdown is a collaborative effort between doctor and patient, and when carried out with skill and empathy on the part of the therapist, the patient is provided with evidence that such interaction can be relatively successful, relatively anxiety-free, and relatively pleasurable. Beyond this point, supportive therapy gradually leads into insight-oriented therapy of schizophrenic patients, a discussion of which, however, is well beyond the scope of this book. The interested student is referred to the monographs by Fromm-Reichmann and by Brody and Redlich (26, 27).

Drug Therapy

In the treatment of schizophrenic patients the tranquilizing drugs are used primarily to control intolerable symptomatology, particularly massive anxiety. A number of other symptoms, such as hallucinations, paranoid delusions, dissociated thought processes, blocking, and impulsive behavior may also respond; but it is thought that this occurs because of reduction of the underlying anxiety rather than because of any specific anti-hallucinatory, anti-delusional, etc., properties of these drugs. We have already mentioned Sullivan's view that intense anxiety in the interpersonal situation is the central disturbance and the basis for much of the secondary elaboration of symptoms (e.g. delusions) in schizophrenia. If this view is correct, we would have a sound rationale for the use of the tranquilizing drugs for schizophrenic patients. It must be admitted, however, that their use was arrived at empirically, not deductively (28).

The phenothiazines, a family of drugs which includes Thorazine, Mellaril, Sparine, Stelazine, and a considerable number of others, have found their greatest usefulness in the treatment of schizophrenic patients. Among them, Thorazine (chlorpromazine) has had the most extensive use; its effects and potential side effects have become well known, and effective dosage ranges have been fairly well established. For these reasons, rather than for any genuine superiority over other phenothiazines, this drug continues to be the favorite of its type among psychiatrists.

The principal therapeutic effect of Thorazine is the reduction of anxiety, even massive anxiety or outright panic. Its major advantage over sedatives is that in dosages which are yet sufficient to control anxiety *it does not affect the sensorium,* that is *it does not produce delirium.* Various other drugs that have been tried in the past—barbiturates, bromides, and other hypnotics—put the patient to sleep or left him chronically delirious.

Drugs of the phenothiazine family are used principally in two situations: to control the massive anxiety (panic) of acute schizophrenic states; to control assaultive or chronically disruptive behavior in chronically hospitalized patients who previously had to be restrained mechanically or secluded.

In acute schizophrenic states Thorazine administered in doses of 100 to 1000 mgm daily (usual dosage is between 200 and 500 mgm daily in acute schizophrenic states) can bring about dramatic changes in the clinical picture. The patient may become calmer, his speech may hang together better and become more meaningful as communication; he may sleep better at night and tolerate the presence of other persons somewhat better. The overall effect seems to be one of a tendency toward reintegration of thought processes, of speech, and of social interaction. Thorazine has its greatest effect in the most acute phase of schizophrenic illness. Usually after several days or weeks the administration of drug is decreased or it may be completely stopped or else administered on a p.r.n. (as needed) basis. For some patients, long-term administration of the drug tends to prevent recurrence of acute psychotic episodes.

Many *chronically assaultive or destructive* patients show a favorable response to the regular or intermittent administration of Thorazine, and although they may still be psychotic in their thinking, their behavior often becomes a great deal more manageable and less disruptive of the total ward setting.

The place of phenothiazine therapy in the treatment of chronically delusional patients is not yet certain. A small percentage of patients improves after several weeks or months of such therapy but many do not. There is also the fact that paranoid patients are often reluctant to accept medication, particularly on a long-term basis.

Side Effects: Numerous side effects are associated with the use of Thorazine, some of which may occur immediately after taking the drug, some others a considerable time after taking the drug. Some responses must be considered idiosyncratic; others have an allergic basis; still others are dose-related.

Hypotension: This may occur immediately after administration of an intramuscular dose of Thorazine or within a half-hour of oral administration of the drug. Placing the patient supine is usually sufficient to re-establish blood pressure. If not, a vasopressor agent can be administered (e.g. Aramine).

Parkinsonism (drug-induced): Mask-like face, stiffness of muscles, even cog-wheel rigidity can be induced in all persons by means of Thorazine administration, but the dose level at which this occurs varies greatly from patient to patient. Anti-Parkinsonian drugs, such as Artane, are effective in counteracting this side effect of Thorazine. *Oculogyric crisis:* Dystonic states of the eye, face, tongue, and neck muscles may occur in a small number of patients receiving phenothiazine drugs. These may mimic epileptic seizures, chorea, or hysterical symptoms. Often the tongue is experienced as enlarged and speech may be affected. The reaction can be dramatically terminated by the intravenous administration of 25 to 50 mgm of Benadryl, or more slowly by oral use of Benadryl or Artane. *Drowsiness:* This occurs in most persons but is usually transient, tending to disappear after two to three days.

Skin rashes and photosensitivity: A measles-like rash, sometimes with itching, occurs in from 5 to 20 per cent of patients taking Thorazine. A peripheral eosinophilia is generally associated with this. When it occurs, Thorazine should be discontinued or another preparation (e.g. Mellaril) substituted. *Jaundice:* A cholangiostatic type of jaundice occurs in a small percentage of patients taking Thorazine. Frequent liver-function tests and close clinical observation should lead to early detection of this complication. The drug must be promptly discontinued. *Agranulocytosis:* This is the most serious complication associated with Thorazine intake. Several fatalities have resulted from it. It is rare but very serious. Differential blood counts at regular intervals may warn of its onset. Infections, particularly fungus infections of the oral cavity, are often a late sign of the existence of agranulocytosis.

Thus, while Thorazine is a very helpful agent, it also has potential dangers. It should not be used in the treatment of mild "neurotic" anxiety.

Other "Somatic" Therapies

The use of *lobotomy* in treating schizophrenic patients has been abandoned in this country as "of no proven value."

The use of *insulin coma therapy* has been abandoned in all but a few psychiatric centers in this country, not because it is necessarily ineffective, but because it seems to be no more effective than electro-convulsive therapy, which is a great deal less troublesome to administer.

Electro-convulsive therapy continues to be used, primarily in two situations: in acute catatonic conditions, either stupor or excitement, and in depression, when it occurs in the course of schizophrenic illness, particularly that variety of depression which has been described under schizo-affective disorder (see Chapter 2). The value of electro-convulsive therapy in other phases of schizophrenia has not been firmly established.

The Course and Outcome of Schizophrenia

Psychiatrists are still very limited in their ability to predict the long-term outcome of psychotic episodes in individual schizophrenic patients. This is so in part because the limits of this disorder, at least in its less typical forms, remain poorly defined. Nevertheless, two types of data have emerged with some consistency:

I. When large groups of patients diagnosed as schizophrenic are studied over long periods of time, the outcomes tend to fall into one of three distinct categories. Approximately one-third will show more or less complete remission from their psychosis after a period of time. A second third will show remissions and exacerbations from time to time, and though this group is able to improve, these patients will need intermittent rehospitalization. The final third of these patients experiences chronic and persistent invalidism as a result of their disorder.

II. A series of factors has been identified which, when present at the time of the examination, tends to presage a more favorable outlook. Some of the most important of these factors are: (1) the illness is of short duration (less than six months); (2) the onset is acute, rather than insidious; (3) major rather than minor precipitating circumstances can be identified; (4) depressive affect and preoccupation with dying is prominent in the presenting symptomatology; (5) perplexity and confusion are present; (6) pre-morbid work, social, and sexual adjustment have been good (29, 30).

Making a prediction about the future course in individual instances is, of course, quite difficult. However, the hopelessness that previously existed about the diagnosis of schizophrenia has been ameliorated. With the aid of psychotherapy, tranquilizing drugs, and intermittent hospitalizations, many such patients can lead reasonably productive, reasonably self-reliant, and at least intermittently satisfying lives.

REFERENCES

1. Eugen Bleuler, *Dementia Praecox or the Group of Schizophrenias,* International Universities Press, New York, 1950.
2. John C. Whitehorn and Barbara Betz, "A Study of Psychotherapeutic Relationships between Physicians and Schizophrenic Patients," *Amer. J. Psychiat.,* 111:321, 1954.
3. Paul E. Meehl, "Schizotaxia, Schizotypy, Schizophrenia," *Amer. Psycholog.,* 17:827–38, 1962.
4. J. S. Kasanin, editor, *Language and Thought in Schizophrenia,* University of California Press, Berkeley, Calif., 1944.
5. Silvano Arieti, *The Interpretation of Schizophrenia,* Brunner, New York, 1955.
6. Harry Stack Sullivan, *Schizophrenia as a Human Process,* Norton, New York, 1962.
7. Ronald D. Laing, *The Divided Self,* Quadrangle Books, Chicago, 1960.
8. Harold F. Searles, *Collected Papers on Schizophrenia and Related Subjects,* International Universities Press, New York, 1965.
9. Emil Kraepelin, *Lehrbuch der Psychiatrie,* seventh edition, Barth, Leipzig, 1903.
10. Sigmund Freud, "Psychoanalytic Notes on an Autobiographical Account of a Case of Paranoia (Dementia Paranoides)," in *Collected Papers,* III, Basic Books, New York, 1959.
11. Harry Stack Sullivan, *Conceptions in Modern Psychiatry,* William A. White Psychiatric Foundation, Washington, 1947.
12. Franz J. Kallman, "The Genetic Theory of Schizophrenia," *Amer. J. Psychiat.,* 103:309–22, 1946.
13. J. R. Smythies, *Schizophrenia,* Charles C. Thomas, Springfield, Ill., 1963.
14. Jacques S. Gottlieb, *et al.,* "Production of High-Energy Phosphate Bonds in Schizophrenia," *Arch. Gen. Psychiat.,* 1:243, 1959.
15. Seymour Kety, "Biochemical Theories of Schizophrenia," *Int. J. Psychiat.,* 1:409–47, 1965.
16. Don D. Jackson, *The Etiology of Schizophrenia,* Basic Books, New York, 1960.
17. Adolf Meyer, "Dynamic Interpretation of Dementia Praecox," *Amer. J. Psychol.,* 21:385, 1910.
18. Gregory Bateson, *et al.,* "Toward a Theory of Schizophrenia, "*Behav. Sci.,* 1:251, 1956.
19. R. W. Lidz and Theodore Lidz, "The Family Environment of Schizophrenia Patients," *Amer. J. Psychiat.,* 106:332, 1949.
20. Dan Greenberg, *How To Be a Jewish Mother,* Price, Stern, and Sloan, Los Angeles, 1964.

21. John H. Weakland and William F. Fry, Jr., "Letters of Mothers of Schizophrenics," *Amer. J. Orthopsychiat.*, 32:604–23, 1962.
22. P. Hoch and P. Polatin, "Pseudoneurotic Forms of Schizophrenia," *Psychiat. Quart.*, 23:248, 1949.
23. P. Hoch, *et al.*, "The Course and Outcome of Pseudoneurotic Schizophrenia," *Amer. J. Psychiat.*, 119:106–15, 1962.
24. Milbank Memorial Fund, *An Approach to the Prevention of Disability from Chronic Psychoses*, Milbank Memorial Fund, New York, 1958.
25. Eric Pfeiffer, "Patients as Therapists," *Amer. J. Psychiat.*, 123:1413–18, 1967.
26. Frieda Fromm-Reichmann, *Principles of Intensive Psychotherapy*, University of Chicago Press, Chicago, 1950.
27. E. B. Brody and F. C. Redlich, editors, *Psychotherapy with Schizophrenics*, International Universities Press, New York, 1952.
28. L. B. Kalinowski and P. H. Hoch, *Somatic Treatments in Psychiatry*, Grune & Stratton, New York, 1961.
29. J. H. Stephens and C. Astrup, "Prognosis in 'Process' and 'Non-Process' Schizophrenia," *Amer. J. Psychiat.*, 119:945–53, 1963.
30. George E. Vaillant, "The Prediction of Recovery in Schizophrenia," *J. Nerv. Ment. Dis.*, 135:534–43, 1962.

4

Organic Brain Disease

We classify as organic brain disorders those states in which impairment of brain-cell function has occurred and in which such impairment is responsible for or associated with detectable impairment of mental functioning, particularly of cognitive functioning. We label as *acute brain syndromes* those states in which impairment of brain tissue functioning is reversible, as *chronic brain syndromes* those states in which impairment is irreversible. These two types of organic brain disease are also commonly referred to as *delirium* and *dementia* respectively.

ACUTE BRAIN SYNDROME OR DELIRIUM

Delirium is a fairly common clinical syndrome. It ranges in severity from very mild disturbances, which can be detected only by highly specialized tests, to frank confusion and disorientation, all the way to coma. Delirium can be caused by many different types of etiologic agents, such as metabolic disorder, circulatory disorder, infection, or intoxication with any one of several hundred possible drugs. Each of these agents does not lead to a separate clinical entity. Rather, certain basic physiological and psychological processes are common to all acute brain syndromes, regardless of which etiologic agent is involved.

In *physiological* terms, delirium represents a state of disordered brain-cell metabolism, or, cerebral insufficiency, as Engel has referred to it, in analogy to renal and hepatic metabolism (1). The electroencephalogram (EEG), which measures electrical activity of the cerebral cortex, serves as a sensitive indicator of the functional integrity of the cortex; and interference with metabolism of the cerebral cortex is reflected in the EEG as a slowing of the alpha wave frequency. In fact, the studies of Engel have indicated that the degree of slowing of the brain wave frequency corresponds closely to the degree of cerebral insufficiency that exists. Thus, when the presence of delirium is suspected on clinical grounds, it can be reliably confirmed or ruled out by obtaining an electroencephalographic tracing. The normal range of alpha wave frequency is between 8 and 12 cycles per second; a frequency below this level is indicative of delirium. However, some persons who are judged to be delirious on clinical (psychological) grounds have EEG frequencies within the accepted range. This does not necessarily rule out delirium. Serial recordings may show that the normal apha wave frequency of such individuals lies at the upper level of the accepted range, and that a slowing in EEG frequency has indeed occurred. To be more precise, it should be stated that what is characteristic of the EEG pattern in delirium is a slowing of the EEG frequency relative to the frequency typical of the individual. Another point which should be mentioned is that serial tracings provide more information than a single tracing.

In *psychological* terms, delirium represents a state of disordered mental functioning, particularly of cognitive functioning. The degree of cognitive deficit corresponds in a rough way to the degree of EEG slowing. Thus, the slowest frequencies will be seen in stuporous or near-stuporous states, while slight slowing will be evident when the cognitive deficit is only slight. As the psychological manifestations of delirium clear, the EEG pattern returns to its pre-morbid frequency concomitantly.

As we have mentioned, the presence of cognitive deficit is the primary psychological sign of delirium. Other disturbances of mental functioning may also be present, such as hallucinations, delusions, or loss of control of aggressive impulses. These secondary manifestations of delirium may be very similar to hallucinations, delusions, or aggressive behavior seen in the so-called functional mental disorders, e.g. in schizophrenia. Presence of cognitive deficit is the differentiating feature.

Some individuals show principally cognitive deficit, with little or no disturbances in other areas of functioning, while others manifest floridly psychotic pictures. Two groups of factors seem to be important for this: One, delirium results in a general weakening of ego functions; ordinarily unacceptable personality traits which have been held in check may under these new circumstances surge to the foreground and significantly influence the clinical picture. Two, the awareness of cognitive deficit has different meanings to different individuals. Loss of ability to think clearly and rationally may be severely disturbing and anxiety provoking to certain individuals whose self-image depends on the intactness of these functions; or on the other hand, cognitive deficit may be accepted quite calmly as a concomitant manifestation of physical illness or other known metabolic disturbance.

The degree of delirium has, of course, a bearing on what the patient experiences and on what the physician observes. When delirium is mild, only a narrow range of cognitive functions is disrupted, while other cognitive functions remain intact. As delirium increases in severity, more and more mental operations become disrupted, resulting finally in a total lack of responsiveness to environmental stimuli, a state we recognize as coma. Coma of course is not merely a psychological state, but one which involves the whole organism.

Early or Mild Manifestations

The mental functions which are most sensitive to a disordering of brain function are as follows: level of awareness of, and ability to appreciate correctly, one's surrounding; ability to concentrate and to perform serial mental tasks; ability to call up at will desired memories and information; precise orientation in time. Difficulties in these areas can be overcome initially by greater voluntary effort, so that an observer may not become aware that the patient is experiencing any difficulty.

Later Manifestations

As delirium deepens, deficit becomes more apparent. Particular difficulty is experienced in ordering past events in the correct temporal sequence. Factual questions are answered in a vague and hesitant manner, and definite memory gaps exist. At this point some patients will experience a reaction which must be regarded as pathognomonic of organic brain disease of recent onset: the so-called catastrophic reaction of Goldstein (2). It occurs, often in the course of mental status examination or sometimes during spontaneous activity, when the patient is suddenly confronted with failure in the performance of mental tasks previously a part of his routine repertory. An example might be the patient who realizes that he is unable to recall his own phone number or that he is unable to perform serial subtraction of 7 from 100. A sudden change will take place. The previously calm patient will become anxious, tremulous, or grossly agitated. Beads of sweat will appear on his forehead and on his palms, and his pupils will become dilated. He may become hostile, belligerent, or negativistic; in any case he will seek to avoid any further questioning. The reaction will gradually subside; but it can be elicited again under similar circumstances. Goldstein's catastrophic reaction represents a failure of adaptive or defensive mechanisms in the face of a difficult task, and a consequent flooding of the individual with massive anxiety. Such reactions are not seen in patients who have carried a cognitive deficit for a long time, for they have developed more effective defenses to cope with the deficit.

Manifestations of Severe Delirium

More severe degrees of delirium are characterized by clear-cut disorientation for time and place. Patients begin to appear confused and bewildered. They misidentify persons and objects, generally along lines of mistaking unfamiliar persons or objects for familiar ones (3). They become unable to comprehend and to follow instructions. They lose interest in their appearance, neglecting to wash or shave. Even simple skills that require the co-ordination of several movements can no longer be carried out. For instance, patients may no longer tie their shoe laces, or they may need to be fed. Increasingly the patients are out of touch with their environment.

Drowsiness gradually increases. Speech becomes slurred, patients may stumble or fall; they become incontinent of stool and urine. Somnolence gradually supervenes and patients ultimately lapse into coma. Delirium of course does not go on to coma in all instances. Any one of the stages of delirium outlined above may represent the maximum severity of delirium for any given patient.

Fluctuating Levels of Awareness

A feature characteristic of delirium at all levels of severity is the tendency toward fluctuation in level of awareness even though the clinical condition causing the delirium is otherwise stable.* For instance, a patient delirious from chronic uremia, might at one moment be totally disoriented for time and place, yet half an hour later be able to give both correctly, and at the same time be unable to recall having been asked about them before. These moment-to-moment fluctuations in level of awareness (or of cognitive deficit generally) are not related to fluctuations in the severity of the physiological deficit. They are thought to reflect

* To a lesser degree the same is true of dementia.

fluctuations in the adequacy of psychological defenses. Some of the factors which seem to have a bearing on this problem can be summed up as follows: cognitive performance in delirium tends to be better in a familiar, benevolent setting, poorer in an unfamiliar or hostile setting. But this statement would be correct for many different kinds of performance, in many different types of clinical situation. Fatigue also seems to play a role here. Still other factors, as yet not elicited, must have a determining influence on this phenomenon.

CAUSES OF DELIRIUM

Intoxication with alcohol, to a mild or more severe degree, is probably the most common cause of delirium, and one with which most adult persons are familiar. A single episode of alcohol intoxication is generally of little clinical significance, only in so far as it may serve as a readily accessible example of a short-lived delirium. During ordinary alcohol intoxication, such as might develop in the course of a Saturday night drinking party, all the features of mild to moderately severe delirium may be observed.

Aside from alcohol, the list of drugs or chemicals which may cause delirium is virtually endless; however, certain drugs are implicated in clinically significant delirium more often than others. Outstanding among these are the following: the hypnotics, particularly the barbiturates, but also paraldehyde, Doriden, chloral hydrate, bromides, etc.; certain of the so-called tranquilizers, especially meprobamate; the narcotics, both naturally occurring (morphine) as well as synthetic (Demerol) types; anti-epileptic drugs (e.g. Dilantin); the amphetamines; atropine; certain of the anti-depressant drugs (e.g. Tofranil); hallucinogenic drugs, such as LSD or peyote. Whenever drugs are involved in the causation of delirium one must look beyond the chemical factors to the personality factors which led to the use of the drug. Many persons with chemically induced delirium have significant neurotic, psychotic, or characterological problems which led to the use of the chemical agents in question. We are concerned here in particular with persons who have a tendency to become addicted or dependent upon drugs, and with persons who have attempted suicide, for any large number of possible reasons, by the ingestion of larger than recommended doses of drug. Among patients admitted directly to psychiatric services, drug intoxication is the most frequent cause of delirium. The same is not true of patients found to be delirious on other medical services.

A second group of causes of delirium consists of a number of metabolic disorders, such as myxedema, hyperthyroidism, pernicious anemia, severe anemia from any cause, and various vitamin deficiencies. The metabolic disorder may be associated not only with delirium but with neurotic and psychotic symptoms as well. In myxedema, for instance, well-developed syndromes of depression or paranoid delusions may be seen in addition to the cognitive deficit (myxedema madness). In general, the delirium responds rapidly to adequate therapy of the basic disturbance.

A third group of causes of delirium consists of a number of major medical diseases. These produce delirium either as a result of circulatory disturbances, of electrolyte imbalance, or of metabolic toxins. Here we would place congestive heart failure, hepatic and renal failure, chronic pulmonary disease (CO_2 retention), diabetic acidosis, and water intoxication. These patients are for the most part severely ill. They make up the largest number of delirious patients seen in psychiatric consultation on medical and surgical services.

Delirium is also a prominent feature of post-convulsive states (including post-ECT states), of central nervous system infections (especially meningitis), of head trauma (concussion, contusion), and of intracranial vascular accidents to the extent that these cause, in addition to actual brain cell necrosis (which is irreversible), such reversible changes as edema, compression, and irritation. This by no means exhausts the list of possible causes of delirium, but should suffice for our purposes.

EXAMINATION OF THE DELIRIOUS PATIENT

Since delirium is a common clinical syndrome, the level of suspicion for the diagnosis should be high. This is true when the patient's presenting symptoms are purely psychological, or when mental symptoms commence in a setting of major medical illness. In the latter situation the possibility of delirium should always be entertained and appropriate tests done to establish or rule out the diagnosis.

Evidence suggesting delirium is usually obtained during the course of routine history-taking. There are two clues one should look for: positive history of drug intake, metabolic disease, blow on the head, epilepsy, infection (compare section on causes of delirium); and positive signs of diminished mental acuity in answering the routine questions of history-taking. Once the examiner's suspicion has been aroused, he will then make the cognitive performance of the patient an object of special study. Since such an examination can be a very threatening experience, especially to patients with cognitive deficit, closer questioning should be deferred until some rapport has been established between doctor and patient. The patient's co-operation is crucial for an accurate assessment of cognitive performance.

In examining for delirium one wishes to test those functions known to be typically impaired in the disorder: orientation; attention; serial or sequential mental operations; recent memory; and visual-motor co-ordination. This is done briefly by asking the patient the time of day, the date and day of the week, by asking whether he knows where he is, and by asking for a chronological account of the events, including times, names, and places, leading up to the present meeting between doctor and patient. In so doing one has checked not only orientation, but also sequential mental operations and recent memory. The request to have the patients subtract 7 serially from 100 is a further check on attention as well as on the ability to perform serial tasks. Some questions about recent news events may yield further information about recent memory and may allow the examiner to guess how long a deficit has existed. A very simple test of visual-motor co-ordination is to ask the patient to write his name; handwriting is quite sensitive to central nervous system disordering. All of these are gross tests but they are immediately available to the clinician. They must be interpreted in the light of what each individual patient might properly be expected to produce, on the basis of information one has about the educational and socio-economic level he has attained. Thus, someone with a third-grade education might be expected to have difficulty with serial 7's, with or without delirium.

When more subtle deficits are suspected or when more precise measurements of degree of organic deficit are required, the services of a clinical psychologist should be sought. He would likely administer subtests of the Wechsler Adult Intelligence Scale, along with the Bender Gestalt test, to pinpoint the presence and degree of cognitive deficit.

TREATMENT OF DELIRIUM

Treatment of the delirious patient consists of *specific* treatment directed toward the correction of the underlying metabolic disturbance (e.g. treatment of congestive heart failure, of diabetic acidosis, or discontinuation of the offending drug) and of *nonspecific*, supportive treatment. The latter consists of maintaining a reassuring, clarifying attitude toward the patient in order to help him understand and accept his current impairment; providing a consistent, structured, and relatively undemanding environment (i.e. a private, quiet, well-lighted room); regular contact with familiar persons; adequate food and fluid intake; avoidance of potentially deliriogenic drugs, such as barbiturates for sedation or for sleep (if drugs must be used to calm a very agitated or disturbed patient, the phenothiazines, e.g. chlorpromazine, are the drugs of choice since they do not produce delirium); closely supervising the patient to prevent him from harming himself, either accidentally or intentionally (a low bed is provided to decrease the danger of falling out of bed). In addition to these general supportive measures, which are applicable to virtually all delirious patients, specific psychotherapeutic measures are sometimes helpful. These are based on an understanding of the personality structure of the patient, and on the specific meaning that the existence of delirium has for the patient.

PROGNOSIS IN DELIRIUM

The outcome of delirium is exceedingly variable. It depends in large part on the nature of the underlying disturbance. Although we have defined delirium as a reversible impairment of brain function, we should now point out that when delirium persists for very long periods or occurs repeatedly, permanent brain damage may result, e.g. in the patient chronically addicted to alcohol. One possible outcome of delirium then may be residual permanent damage or dementia, of varying degrees. A second possible outcome is complete clearing of the delirium without any residual cognitive deficit and a total reintegration of the personality. An instance of this might be the febrile delirium associated with a severe pneumonia in an otherwise healthy person. A third possible outcome may be persistence of a potentially reversible brain syndrome, such as in chronic uremia or in chronic bromide intoxication which either goes undetected or untreated. A fourth and indeed quite frequent outcome of acute brain syndromes is death. Death may result either as a direct effect of the toxic agent or drug (e.g. a massive overdose of barbiturates) or as a result of the underlying medical disease. Delirium is often associated with or the result of very serious medical illness, and the prognosis of the delirium is then the prognosis of the medical illness.

A few further remarks about terminology in organic brain disorder need to be made in an attempt to clarify an area of possible confusion. Reversible organic brain syndromes may either be short-lived, which is the more usual case, or they may exist for months or even years and thus deserve to be called chronic. In order to avoid having to call something "chronic acute brain syndrome," we suggest the term "chronic delirium." The clinical picture in chronic delirium is the same as that which we ordinarily consider as characteristic of dementia; that is, while a cognitive deficit of a certain severity clearly exists, the individual has over a period of time developed fairly effective ways of covering up such a deficit, from himself and from others. By the same token, dementia may develop acutely and thus show clinical manifestations which we ordinarily consider as characteristic of delirium and yet be of a permanent nature. Again, in order to avoid the paradoxical term "acute chronic brain syndrome" (i.e. acute irreversible brain syndrome) we prefer the term "acute dementia." Clearly, two different concepts are involved: reversibility vs. irreversibility; acuteness vs. chronicity. While the former is of greater significance in determining prognosis, the latter is of greater significance in determining clinical manifestations.

DEMENTIA OR CHRONIC BRAIN SYNDROME

Delirium and dementia are the two major groups of psychiatric disorders which have a clearly established organic basis. To all other psychiatric disorders we ascribe, at least in our present state of knowledge, a non-organic, "functional," or psychogenic origin. We have defined delirium as a reversible organic brain disorder and dementia as an irreversible one. While this represents the main differentiating feature, other differences also obtain between the two types of disorders in regard to their clinical picture, physiology, psychology, etiology, prognosis and treatment. Yet in each of these areas the two types of disorders are related one to the other, and throughout this presentation we will try to keep the features of both in mind for comparison.

Dementia, like delirium, is a common disorder. It occurs primarily in the older age groups, while delirium is as likely to occur in the young as it is in the old. Delirium is usually of short duration, while dementia on the whole runs a protracted course. Hence, many demented patients ultimately find their way into public mental hospitals for prolonged care.

We have stated that dementia is associated with old age. As life expectancy has increased in the last half-century, more and more persons live to an old age, and hence are exposed to the risk of dementia. As a consequence the prevalence of dementia has increased greatly in the last several decades. At the present time, dementia is the leading cause of first admissions to state hospitals, and it ranks second, behind chronic schizophrenia, in the resident population of state hospitals. This interesting reversal between dementia and schizophrenia as the first and second leading diagnoses among first admissions and in the resident population is accounted for by the fact that the life expectancy of chronic schizophrenic patients at the time of their admissions is far greater than that of demented patients; i.e. each schizophrenic patient spends, on the average, many more patient-years in the hospital than does each demented patient; this leads to an accumulation of schizophrenic cases in the resident population.

Dementia is a clinical syndrome caused by or associated with loss of functioning brain tissue. It is a general syndrome which can be caused by a variety of etiologic agents or processes. Each of these agents or processes does not result in a separate clinical entity. Unfortunately, the authors of most textbooks of psychiatry have proceeded to discuss specific types of dementia *as separate clinical entities,* omitting, or providing only very sketchy, discussions of the general syndrome (4). Some general features of dementia that transcend all varieties of dementia should be recognized.

PATHOPHYSIOLOGY OF DEMENTIA

In physiological terms, dementia represents an insufficiency syndrome based on the loss of functioning brain substance. The brain is the organ of adaptation. As such it is a highly specialized and differentiated organ. It does not have the capacity to regenerate. This means that brain cells which for one reason or another have died, cannot be replaced. But the brain, too, like other organs, has a certain amount of reserve capacity; that is, it can tolerate a certain amount of loss of tissue without significant loss of function. Tissue destruction beyond this margin of safety (and this margin of safety is much narrower for the brain than it is for liver or kidney, for instance) results in failure of adaptation. When tissue destruction has occurred diffusely throughout the brain, this failure of adaptation will manifest itself primarily in the psychological sphere; when it is more highly localized, psychological as well as neurological impairment may result.

A number of techniques are available to evaluate the presence, extent, and severity of brain cell destruction. One of these is the electroencephalographic tracing (EEG). While it provides reliable information in evaluating the presence of delirium, it is far less reliable in helping to establish a diagnosis of dementia. Well-established dementia of mild to moderate severity is often associated with either a normal brain wave pattern or one which shows only slight slowing. Localized areas of non-functioning brain tissue on the other hand are reflected more accurately in EEG tracings, either as focal slowing of the brain wave or as foci of heightened (irritative foci) activity. In severe dementia the EEG pattern is characterized by slowing of frequency and decrease in voltage so as to very nearly approach a straight line record.

The pneumoencephalogram (PEG) is a second technique which finds some application in the detection of loss of brain tissue. When diffuse loss of brain cells has occurred, the brain shrinks. This leads to compensatory enlargement of the fluid spaces within (ventricles) and around (subarachnoid spaces) the brain. Injection of air into these spaces permits their visualization and recognition of enlargement if such has occurred. This technique is primarily applicable in establishing the diagnosis of pre-senile dementia.

A number of other techniques are also used to evaluate brain pathology: lumbar puncture, brain scan, skull X-rays, cerebral angiography, visual field examination, and even, brain biopsy. These are often of greater value in determining either the specific localization (angiography, brain scan) or the specific character (biopsy) of the brain pathology, rather than in documenting the presence or absence of dementia.

In addition to these highly specialized techniques, a complete neurological examination is always indicated in patients suspected of being demented. Although negative neurological findings do not rule out dementia, positive findings may point to such specific affectations of the central nervous system as are frequently associated with dementia (e.g. brain tumor).

Psychopathology of Dementia

In psychological terms, dementia is a syndrome of permanently impaired brain function. Its clinical psychological manifestations vary not only with the severity of the physiological insufficiency but also with the rapidity with which it develops and with the ability of the individual to cope with the emerging deficit. The last of these accounts for the great variability in the over-all picture.

When the defect is mild, only the highest intellectual functions may be impaired, that is, the ability to abstract, to change set, to assimilate new information. As deficit increases, gross disorientation for time and place, forgetfulness, and memory gaps appear. In other words, while the defect is manifested initially as an inability to adapt to new and changing situations, later the ability to deal with familiar situations and problems is also eroded. Later still, and as a consequence of the same physiological process, gross personality deterioration occurs. At this point even the most basic adaptive functions, such as eating, walking, and control of elimination, can no longer be carried out. When this happens death is near and comes about, either through progress of the disease underlying the dementia, or through intercurrent infection which can no longer be handled adequately by an organism whose adaptive functions are failing.

The comments above on the nature and course of dementia are essentially abstractions. We will now turn to the clinical observations which can commonly be made on demented patients, and on which the abstractions are based. For purposes of exposition it will be useful to divide the clinical course of dementia into three stages: beginning dementia; fully developed dementia; deterioration.

Beginning Dementia

The onset of dementia is often gradual. When this is so the initial presenting features of the illness may not be obvious intellectual deficit as one might suspect, but rather a variety of emotional or behavioral changes. Depression, loss of interest, fatigue, listlessness, anxiety, or agitation are often seen in the early stages of dementia. These symptoms may result in a diagnosis of a "functional" neurosis or psychosis. Personality changes are also seen. Irritability, social withdrawal, emotional outbursts, inconsiderateness, petulance, moral laxity, and irregular work attendance are frequent in the history of patients with early dementia. At times these changes are present for months or years before anyone in the patient's surroundings notices any clear-cut memory deficit, confusion, or disorientation. Nevertheless, even at this stage, careful mental status examination or formal psychological testing reveals impairment of abstraction, attention, concentration, retention of recently learned material, and, particularly, retention and reproduction of geometric designs involving visual-motor co-ordination (Bender-Gestalt test).

At this stage some patients are aware of the specific difficulties they are experiencing. Others are aware in a very general way that "something is wrong" but cannot identify the difficulty any further. They may focus on somatic concerns or may project their difficulties onto their job situations, onto minority groups, or onto the world situation. Anxiety, concern, and perplexedness are experienced to a greater or lesser degree by most persons who are developing dementia. The individual's previous life adjustment, his expectations and his valuation of intellectual abilities, his previous experience with dementia in friends or relatives play an important role in how he will adjust to his difficulty. He may deny it, he may resist it and try to adapt in spite of it, or he may give up. Equally important as an individual's own reaction to his dementia is the reaction of those close to him—his spouse, relatives, employers, friends. If he is rejected by them because of his changed condition, his self-esteem will be further eroded, and his over-all adaptive capacity further compromised.

Fully Developed Dementia

When dementia becomes fully developed there is usually little difficulty in recognizing the syndrome. A recent study by Babigian *et al.* (5) shows that dementia can be more reliably diagnosed than any other group of psychiatric disorders. Different psychiatrists, examining the same patient at different times, will arrive at the same diagnosis more frequently than is the case with any other type of psychiatric disorder. Memory loss, confusion, disorientation, forgetfulness, are some of the classic signs of dementia. Patients may appear confused and bewildered. They may wander away from home and hardly know that they are lost. Their judgment is poor in regard to financial matters, in matters of social probity, or in regard to the feelings of others. They themselves may take offense more easily than was previously their custom; they show emotional lability and sudden outbursts of anger or irritation; they may be stubborn and hard to please. They pay less and less attention to personal appearance and cleanliness.

Sleep patterns are often disturbed, with patients experiencing daytime drowsiness and nighttime restlessness. A certain number of patients develop secondary psychotic symptoms in the form of paranoid or grandiose delusions and hallucinations. The greatest significance of these last-named symptoms rests with the fact that such manifestations are less understandable and less acceptable to families than is simple forgetfulness. Their occurrence may lead to extrusion of the demented person from the family home. Nursing homes too, though housing large numbers of "simple" demented persons, have a low tolerance for clear-cut psychotic manifestations and may insist on having such patients committed to state institutions.

Persons with dementia of long standing usually develop a number of characteristic defensive mechanisms to help them deal with their cognitive deficit. These are, on the one hand, adaptive in that they avoid anxiety for the individual by denying or covering up the cognitive deficit; they are maladaptive in that they either represent a break with reality or else narrow the range of activity to such a degree as to exclude all but the most familiar. The list of these defenses includes confabulation, denial, perseveration, avoidance, negativism, jocularity, diversion maneuvers of every kind, bantering, and provocation (6). They are employed primarily in unfamiliar (hence threatening) situations in which their mental capacity is likely to be either strained or put to the test. The confrontation by a stranger or the usual mental status examination by a medical student may serve as examples of such situations.

Confabulation is probably the best known of these mechanisms. Historically it has been associated almost exclusively with Korsakoff's psychosis, i.e. the chronic organic brain syndrome associated with chronic alcohol intoxication. However, confabulation may be observed in dementia from any cause, if only the disorder is not too severe (i.e. deterioration has not yet occurred) and sufficient time has elapsed for this intriguing defense mechanism to develop. Confabulation consists in the production of fictitious memories, often with fanciful or elaborate detail, to fill in gaps in memory or to round out an incompletely understood situation. Confabulation can occur spontaneously, or it may be elicited by asking questions of the patient while giving him to understand that the examiner expects him to know the answers.

Another very interesting coping device characteristic of long-standing cognitive deficit is perseveration. Perseveration may be observed in any area of psychomotor activity, speech, writing, drawing, locomotion. It is a graphic demonstration of a demented person's difficulty in changing set, clinging instead to familiar activities. Examples of this might be the retelling of the same story, in full detail, to be sure, over and over. Or for an example in another sphere: A man was asked to write the sentence, Now is the time for all good men to come to the aid of their party. He wrote: "Now is the time time t t t t t t t," finally trailing off the page.

Some of the other techniques of dealing with cognitive deficit can be illustrated briefly: A demented man is asked to subtract 7 from 100. He replies: "Now, you've asked me a lot of questions, Doc, now I'm going to ask you some questions. Who won the World Series in 1935? Who? Who?" An old woman, asked to perform the same task, replied: "Well, you have a lot of nerve young man, asking an old woman a lot of foolish questions."

The presence of such defensive mechanisms indicates two things: the intellectual deficit has been present for some considerable period of time; the ego is not overwhelmed by the deficit, but is still trying to adapt to it.

Deterioration

If the dementing process continues, patients will gradually enter a period of decline and deterioration. Patients become increasingly dependent for their needs on others and at this stage need constant supervision. Their speech becomes either monosyllabic or deteriorates into meaningless mumbles, so that they can no longer express their needs verbally. Motor control too falters. They can no longer feed themselves, dress themselves, or go to the toilet, and the initiative for these activities has by this time long disappeared. Ultimately the patient progresses toward a stage of namelessness, that is, he may either not know his own name or may no longer respond to his name. Knowing one's own name is one of the last abilities to become impaired, and this is seen only in the severe forms of dementia. When the patient finally becomes bedridden, and when he can no longer control his sphincters, intercurrent infections, either septicemia from decubitus ulcer formations or hypostatic pneumonia, develop and terminate the patient's life.

SPECIFIC SUBTYPES OF DEMENTIA

Senile Brain Disease

Two statements have been made regarding old age: That if men lived long enough they would all develop senile dementia. That old men retain their intellects well enough if they keep their minds active and fully employed. These views, although mutually incompatible, both express important truths, but *the* truth falls somewhere between. While it is true that most men who live long enough will develop the pathological changes of senile brain disease, not all of them will develop the clinical features of dementia. Put another way, the correlation between clinical symptomatology and pathological derangement is very imperfect when it comes to senile brain disease. On the other hand it appears from clinical studies that persons who have "fewer resources" or who have had a precarious life adjustment prior to reaching old age, are more likely to show the clinical signs of dementia than are those who have been well adjusted, secure, useful, and productive citizens and who continue to function, even in their old age in challenging and productive endeavors. It seems that such persons have a greater "reserve capacity," a greater capacity to make do with what is left.

The pathological changes in the brain which constitute senile brain disease are a diffuse dropping out of nerve cells, with an increase in glial cells, and formation of diffusely distributed "senile placques," microscopic coalescences of cell debris. On gross examination the brain is shrunken in size, with a widening of sulci and leveling of the gyri. Some compensatory enlargement of the ventricles is usually also present. The cause of the degeneration of brain cells is not known, but it is assumed that it represents a manifestation of the aging process in general. It is of interest that similar atrophy occurs in other organs of the body in persons with senile brain disease, that is, there is shrinkage of muscles, of heart size, and of elastic tissue throughout the body. It is likely that senile brain disease is a manifestation of a more generalized involuting process, with the effect on the brain being the most pronounced.

The clinical psychological manifestations of senile brain disease are those of a regularly advancing dementia. At least initially the clinical picture seems to be little more than an exaggeration of those features which we associate with "normal aging," that is, a narrowing of interest, increasing withdrawal from social contact, mounting self-centeredness, decreased ability to cope with stress and frustration. Thereafter, patients will show all the gradations of intellectual and personality disorganization and, finally, deterioration, much as we have described these features in discussing the general syndrome of dementia. At times, the regular progression of dementia is punctuated by intercurrent episodes of psychosis or even by continued psychosis. Patients may become anxious, depressed, agitated, or violent; they may develop florid auditory or visual hallucinations and fixed or fluctuating delusional schemes. These phenomena are not merely the meaningless by-product of the deterioration of the adaptive organ; when studied closely they express, much in the same manner as dreams and the psychotic symptoms of schizophrenic patients do, concerns, anxieties, and hopes of the individual. They cannot be considered the inevitable concomitant of brain degeneration. The content of the psychotic production may give clues to the nature of the patient's concerns and form a sound basis on which to base a patient's treatment or management.

Dementia Associated with Cerebral Arteriosclerosis

The distinguishing features of dementia associated with cerebral arteriosclerosis are to be understood on the basis of a brain pathology that differs from that found in senile brain disease. The primary defect is occlusive disease of the blood vessels supplying the brain, which results secondarily in brain tissue destruction. Occlusive vascular disease in the brain, as elsewhere, proceeds in general in a stepwise fashion, cutting off the blood supply first to one, then to another area of brain tissue. The resultant clinical symptomatology accordingly shows a stepwise progression of dementia, with gradual improvements and sudden worsenings, as well as stepwise occurrence of localizing neurological signs which, too, may show gradual improvements and sudden worsening. Thus the diagnosis of dementia associated with cerebral arteriosclerosis is based on the presence of dementia, a history of stepwise exacerbation of intellectual deficit, and the presence or history of presence of localizing neurological defects. Evidence of arteriosclerosis elsewhere in the body is supporting but not sufficient evidence for making the diagnosis, since the progress of arteriosclerosis may be proceeding at different rates in different parts of the body. It has been observed that there is a greater degree of emotional lability in persons dementing from cerebral arteriosclerosis than is seen in senile brain disease. This fact finds its explanation in the successively repeated and unexpected onslaughts on the organ of adaptation, as contrasted with the gradual decline of adaptive functions in persons with senile dementia.

On the average the age of persons with arteriosclerotic dementia is somewhat lower (55–70) than is that for persons with senile dementia (65–80), but the spread is wide for both groups.

Pre-Senile Dementia

The age period from 45–60 has been, somewhat arbitrarily, described as the pre-senium. In it three "distinct" types of dementia have their onset: Alzheimer's disease, Pick's disease, and Jakob-Creutzfeldt disease, in decreasing order of frequency of occurrence. While they can be distinguished one from the other on clinical grounds (i.e. in life), their differentiation is more readily made on the basis of autopsy examination. For our purposes here, however, they will be discussed as a group. Both pathologically and histologically they are related to senile dementia, that is, they represent for the most part a diffuse degeneration of brain cells distributed widely throughout the cortex. This leads to shrinkage of the total brain weight and compensatory enlargement of the ventricles of the brain. The onset of clinical psychological manifestations is in general insidious since at this stage subtle changes in personality (such as the decrease in work performance or in general level of interest) are more apparent than are intellectual deficits. This results not infrequently in an initial diagnosis of a "functional" disorder, such as depression, anxiety reaction, or involutional psychosis. The diagnosis of dementia is associated primarily with old age and hence, "functional" diagnoses are frequently offered when symptoms first develop. The diagnosis can be made when it is suspected, even in early stages with the help of careful mental status examination or psychological testing. Positive findings of a gradual progressive intellectual deficit do not suffice to make the diagnosis. Other possible causes for dementia in this age group must be ruled out by the appropriate studies: lumbar puncture, EEG, skull films, brain scan. Other possible causes are: primary or secondary neoplasm of the brain,

brain abscess, general paresis, or a chronic delirium on the basis of drug or metabolic intoxication.

General Paresis or Dementia Associated with CNS Syphilis

A second type of dementia which usually has its onset this side of the senium is that associated with central nervous system (CNS) syphilis. The entity is of historical as well as clinical interest, for general paresis of the insane, or GPI, as it was called, became the first psychiatric disorder for which an etiology could be discovered and a brain pathology described. Although the increasingly successful methods of treating syphilis (Salvarsan (arsphenamine), arsenicals, malarial fever therapy, and most recently penicillin) have reduced the incidence of syphilis, and hence of late complications of CNS syphilis, general paresis has not disappeared altogether.

General paresis is a late complication of syphilitic infection at an earlier age. It occurs in some 5 per cent of patients whose initial infection goes untreated or is treated inadequately. Its clinical psychological manifestations occur usually some 10 to 15 years after the initial infection. Pathologically, general paresis represents a meningo-encephalitis, i.e. inflammatory lesions are seen distributed throughout the meninges as well as throughout the brain substance.

Classic descriptions of general paresis often contain a statement to the effect that the clinical manifestations of paresis can be identical to that of any other psychiatric disorder, such as anxiety, hysteria, depression, schizophrenia, or mania. Such accounts will often go on to say, "Know thou syphilis and thou knowest the whole of clinical psychiatry," paraphrasing Osler's famous dictum regarding syphilis. This statement is no more true of syphilis than it is of any other type of dementia, or of delirium for that matter. What is true is that certain symptoms, such as euphoria or massive denial, may also be seen in paresis. But in paresis these symptoms (i.e. mania or "bizarre" hallucinations) are always accompanied by evidence of intellectual deficit. Another way of stating this would be to say that the paretic patient has available to him similar psychological mechanism as do other persons. The paretic patient may employ these to deal with his brain function deficit as another person might deal with a conflictual love relationship or with homosexual conflict. The studies of Hollos and Ferenczi, for instance, have demonstrated beautifully that the content of the production of the paretic patients is not meaningless but is determined by the individual's conflicts and concerns, much as are the productions of schizophrenic patients, for example (7).

It is probably true that the clinical picture of the dementias associated with CNS syphilis is more varied than that of other types of dementia. A hypomanic picture with euphoria, grandiose delusions, and expansive behavior is thought of as most typical of the paretic. Such a picture may be seen in perhaps 25 per cent of paretic patients. Another fairly large group of patients shows prominent persecutory delusions, and probably the largest number of patients follow what might best be called an uncomplicated or "simple" dementing course.

One may speculate why euphoria and grandiosity should be more prominently seen in dementia due to syphilis than when it is due to other causes. Euphoria in general is a manifestation of the prominent use of denial. It is possible that dementia due to syphilis has to be more vigorously denied (because of the social unacceptability of syphilis) than when it is due to other causes.

Korsakoff's Psychosis

Korsakoff's psychosis is a chronic brain syndrome associated with protracted nutritional deficiency, particularly, vitamin deficiency (8). As such, it occurs primarily among alcoholics in our culture, though it can be the outcome of nutritional deficiency from any cause. In about 50 per cent of cases the dementia is associated with polyneuritis from the same cause, viz. vitamin deficiency. Korsakoff's psychosis in alcoholics usually does not occur until after many years of excessive drinking coupled with inadequate food intake. Although its onset is usually insidious, sometimes it is first recognized after a bout of delirium tremens. Whether alcohol per se plays any direct role in bringing about brain cell degeneration is not known, nor is the role of delirium tremens or of convulsions associated with D.T.s understood. Since the same type of syndrome can be seen in non-alcoholics it is generally held that the major damage is caused by inadequate nutrition.

In Korsakoff's psychosis a diffuse type of brain cell degeneration occurs. Recent evidence presented by Victor, however, indicates that in addition highly localized areas of degeneration occur in the brain which are thought to represent "memory pathways," such as the mammillo-thalamic tract (9). This may account for the fact that memory seems to be differentially affected to a greater degree than are the other intellectual functions. It may also account for the hypertrophied development of confabulation (pseudo-reminiscences) in these patients to deal with the specific memory defect.

Apart from these specific features mentioned, the clinical manifestations of this type of dementia do not differ significantly from other dementias.

References

1. George L. Engel and John Romano, "Delirium, a Syndrome of Cerebral Insufficiency," *J. Chron. Dis.*, 9:260–77, 1959.
2. Kurt Goldstein, "Functional Disturbances in Brain Damage," pp. 770–94, in *American Handbook of Psychiatry*, Basic Books, New York, 1959.
3. M. Levin, "Delirious Disorientation, the Law of the Unfamiliar Mistaken for the Familiar," *J. Ment. Sci.*, 91:447–53, 1945.
4. Arthur P. Noyes and Lawrence C. Kolb, *Modern Clinical Psychiatry*, fifth edition, Saunders, Philadelphia, 1958.
5. H. M. Babigian, *et al.*, "Diagnostic Consistency and Change in a Follow-Up of 1215 Patients," *Amer. J. Psychiat.*, 121:895–901, 1965.
6. Edwin Weinstein and Robert Kahn, *The Denial of Illness*, Charles C. Thomas, Springfield, Ill., 1955.

7. S. Hollos and S. Ferenczi, *Psychoanalysis of the Psychic Disorder of General Paresis*, Nerv. Ment. Dis. Publications, New York, 1925.

8. M. Victor and P. J. Yakovlev, "S. S. Korsakoff's Psychic Disorder in Conjunction with Peripheral Neuritis, A Translation of the Original Article," *Neurol.*, 5:394–406, 1955.

9. M. Victor, *et al.*, "Memory Loss with Lesions of Hippocampal Formation. Report of a Case with Some Remarks on the Anatomical Basis of Memory," *Arch. Neurol.*, 5:244–63, 1961.

5

Neurotic Behavior

A brief chapter on neurotic behavior cannot do justice to the variety of human behavior which can be so identified, nor to the vast amount of practical and theoretical work which has been expended in the elucidation of the nature of neurotic behavior. Therefore, the current attempt will be limited to an introduction to the phenomenology of neurotic behavior and to a beginning synthesis, based on a variety of sources, of the meaning and causes of neurotic behavior. Throughout we will also want to consider the relationships which exist between neurotic and non-neurotic behavior, as well as between the various forms of neurotic behavior.

A thorough review of underlying theoretical concepts would be desirable. Unfortunately, we cannot point to any one volume or publication where this is done concisely and in a manner which would bring consensus from the experts in this field. Instead we will mention several volumes which, taken together, touch on the most important contributions to this problem. For a strictly psychoanalytic point of view we can do no better than to refer the reader to Fenichel's scholarly standard work on the theory of the neuroses (1). For a somewhat more flexible approach the works of Sullivan should be considered, particularly his *Conceptions of Modern Psychiatry* (2). And for an integration of psychoanalytic and developmental approaches (with a special emphasis on the work of Piaget), Engel's *Psychological Development in Health and Disease,* already referred to in the Preface, is recommended (3).

NEUROTIC BEHAVIOR DEFINED

What constitutes *neurotic behavior?* We have already defined *behavior* as the sum of a person's thoughts, feelings, and actions. It remains for us to define the term "neurotic." Unfortunately, it has more than one definition. One way it is sometimes used, particularly by lay persons, indicates disapproval. Behavior which is troublesome, distasteful, hard to understand, or out of tune with one's own value system, may be referred to as neurotic. In this use of the term there is no regard for the possible mental mechanisms underlying such behavior; it is not used descriptively or by way of explanation, but as a value judgment. For instance, one may hear it said of someone: "He is nothing but a damned neurotic." Naturally, we do not advocate this loose use of the term, but mention it only as an indication of the unfavorable response from the environment that is a fairly regular concomitant of what is thought to be neurotic behavior.

A second way the term "neurotic" is sometimes used is to refer to behavior that is the manifestation of one of the classic psychoneuroses—of hysteria, of phobias, or of obsessive-compulsive neuroses. This narrow use of the term will not be adhered to in this book, although the specific patterns of neurotic behavior mentioned will be discussed, among others, in some detail below.

A third way in which the term "neurotic" is used is to indicate relative severity of emotional disturbance. Used in this sense, *neurotic* behavior is contrasted with *psychotic* behavior. The latter implies more severe personality disintegration, a more primitive mental organization, a greater disregard for reality, and greater over-all disability than is usually seen with neurotic behavior. This method of differentiation is, however, only generally valid, and many exceptions exist. Certain forms of neurotic behavior may be profoundly incapacitating (for instance, severe compulsive disorders), while in others reality may be ignored or pushed aside (as in certain fears of perfectly harmless objects or situations).

Finally, we come to our use of the term "neurotic." As primarily used in this book, the word "neurotic" refers to *behavior which is qualitatively distinct in that it is conflictually motivated and in that it is further characterized by being excessively rigid, inflexible, or stereotyped, unconsciously motivated and therefore not within the full control of the individual, reflexive rather than reflective, and which is, as a result of all of these, maladaptive, self-defeating, and productive of personal suffering.* It should be noted that at this point we have as yet made no mention of the specific thoughts, feelings, or actions which may be considered neurotic. Certain acts or feelings may or may not be neurotic depending on the specific meaning they have for the individual, while certain other acts or feelings almost always indicate neurotic mechanisms at work. For instance, feelings of anger or feelings of sadness in certain situations may be either neurotic or non-neurotic, while an uncontrollable urge to wash one's hands repeatedly or a discomfiting fear of open spaces is always neurotic.

NEUROSES AND PERSONALITY DISORDERS

In this chapter we will discuss *neurotic behavior* as a single category. Disordered behavior is not infrequently classified into two separate categories, viz. *neuroses* and *personality disorders.* In our judgment they are intimately related from a motivational or a dynamic point of view, and the differences between them are differences of form rather than substance. Throughout the chapter we will have ample opportunity to demonstrate this relationship. Fenichel takes a similar view of the relation of one to the other when he refers to the neuroses as *symptom neuroses* and to the personality disorders as *character neuroses* (1). Neuroses are focal disturbances of psychological functioning. In the personality disorders the emotional disturbances are woven into the fabric of the personality.

PERSONALITY: DEFINITION AND FUNCTION

Any definition of personality should be able to accommodate normal personality development and structure and their neurotically disordered counterparts. *Personality, or character,** may be defined as *an individual's typical mode of reacting, in strange as well as in familiar situations.* Personality is the more or less automatically functioning self-system which relates the individual to his environment. It develops out of the person's life experience and out of his constitutional heritage. *It represents the structuralization*** *of his experience at conflict and problem solving, acquired during his entire lifetime, with particular importance attributed to early learned patterns of conflict or problem solving.* It also includes the individual's capacity to *adapt in conflict-free* (4) *areas of psychological functioning,* that is, it takes in motor and sensory apparatuses, intelligence, memory functions, perceptions, and the ability to integrate and organize the multitude of stimuli received from the internal and external environment. Personality is always a mixture of what is commonly human and uniquely individual about a person. The basic function of the personality—to establish and maintain relatedness to the environment—is the same whether we are dealing with normally developed or neurotically disordered personalities. The quality of this relatedness differs, however, so that in the one case it will

---

* In the psychiatric literature the terms *personality* and *character* are sometimes used interchangeably. There can be no objection to this so long as it is realized that whereas in layman's usage the term "character" has the implication of strong moral fiber, in psychiatric usage no such value judgment is implied.

** A psychological function, such as problem solving, if performed repeatedly, in more or less the same manner, becomes a psychological structure, that is, a more or less automatically functioning mechanism for dealing with that particular problem whenever it occurs.

result in satisfaction and pleasure for the individual, in the other case in discontentment and personal suffering.

The Causes of Neurotic Behavior

We now need to go on to a consideration of the root causes of neurotic behavior. Although some investigators still believe that neurotic behavior, or at least the predisposition for its development, can be inherited genetically, we will here go with the majority and assume that neurotic behavior is for the most part caused by unfortunate life experiences with other people. We will further assume that experiences early in life are of greater significance to over-all personality development than experiences later on, but not of so much greater significance that later experiences are not thoroughly capable of modifying personality in major ways. We believe that the evidence is convincing that the human capacity to learn—and by this we mean learning to adapt, as well as learning to solve mathematical problems, learning of names and faces, etc.—is greater than that of any other animal, that it is present very early in life, and continues to flourish into advanced old age.

Conflict and Anxiety

These two concepts, internal conflict and anxiety, stand in the center of most psychological formulations of the causes of neurotic behavior. *Internal conflict* in adult life is generally regarded as a result of patterns of interpersonal conflict early in childhood. *Anxiety* is generally regarded as the result of intrapersonal or interpersonal conflict and also the driving force behind the formation of neurotic symptoms.

Neurotic Anxiety

Anxiety is an unpleasant feeling state, closely related to fear.

It is an uneasy state of mind, a state of psychological arousal, of dread anticipation, but without any clear-cut understanding of what is actually dreaded. It is also a state of physiological arousal, manifested by heightened muscle tension, by rapid heart rate, increased blood pressure, accelerated respiration, and by other signs of sympathetic nervous system overactivity. It is a mental and physiological state anticipating great danger, fight or flight, and possible injury. But what is there to be afraid of? Who is there to fight or to run away from? Many answers have been offered to these questions, none entirely satisfactory. The answer that we find to be in closest congruence with clinical facts holds that in civilized society, except at times of war, the enemy for the most part lies within. In neurotic anxiety what is feared, and what is impossible to run away from, is *disapproval of oneself by "significant others,"* as Sullivan put it (5). Man is a social animal and he depends for his basic humanness on his relatedness with other people.

Let us look at anxiety from another point of view. Engel described it as one of the "primary affects of unpleasure" (6). He further called it "one of the signal-scanning affects," an affect which provides a moment-to-moment answer to man's continual question of "How am I doing?" For the most part, anxiety functions as a "silent signal," just below conscious awareness. It acts as a kind of governor, as a small warning light. As soon as a situation is not going well, that is, not going according to the expectations of the individual, a signal amount of anxiety is elicited, which may make itself felt in a minimal way and at the same time cause the individual to initiate some kind of corrective action appropriate to the situation. If the adjustment is successful, anxiety disappears altogether and in the ordinary course of events may not even be particularly remembered. If the corrective behavior chosen does not in fact improve the situation, however, then the level of anxiety rises considerably and makes itself felt as overtly experienced anxiety. It becomes then, not a gentle warning signal but a jarring alarm. Once anxiety becomes overt and marked, the chances of successful further corrective action are much diminished. In its presence the free choice among available alternatives becomes markedly inhibited and action becomes reflexive rather than reflective. In short, the individual may lose conscious control of the situation in which he finds himself involved. Frequent repetition of this latter pattern of overtly experienced anxiety is of course what we recognize as neurotic behavior.

Let us illustrate: A speaker is giving a lecture to an audience. After a few minutes he notices that some of the people in the back of the room are shifting about uncomfortably. He experiences a minimal (signal) amount of anxiety, and asks himself what might be the trouble. He quickly decides that perhaps he cannot be heard in the back of the room. He therefore inquires whether that is so and learns that that is in fact the trouble. He makes an effort to speak louder, and for the remainder of his lecture his entire audience is attentive, and he is comfortable.

Let us say that another speaker, after the same few minutes, notices the same restlessness in his audience. He, too, experiences a minimal amount of anxiety and he asks himself what might be the trouble. What comes to his mind first, on the basis of his self-concept and past experience, is that the audience does not like him, that they feel that he is not doing a good job. These thoughts intensify his anxiety to noticeable levels, but he still tries to take some corrective action. He decides that instead of speaking freely, using his notes only as a guide, he will read his notes in order not to get lost. As he begins to read, the restlessness in the audience increases. He begins to mispronounce words, a fact of which he of course quickly becomes aware, and his anxiety rises to near-panic level. He may have to break off his lecture, or he and his audience will suffer through the remainder of the time, each breathing a sigh of relief when the ordeal is over.

For the neurotic person there are many such ordeals, and one failure tends to usher in the succeeding one. That is in fact what is meant when we refer to the "vicious spiral of neurotic behavior"—each experience with an unfortunate outcome such as the one we have described makes unfortunate outcomes in future interactions all the more likely. It is in this sense that neurotic behavior is self-perpetuating.

Neurotic Conflict

Neurotic conflict, as we meet it in adult patients, is primarily internal, i.e. intrapersonal, conflict. It comes into being as the result of internalization * of what was previously *conflict between people,* particularly between a child and his parents (or parent substitutes). Specifically, it is the result of *unresolved interpersonal conflict,* constituting *unfinished business held over from childhood.* It is a continuing struggle between the natural instinctual drives of the person and those parts of the personality which forbid or inhibit them. These latter restraining influences, in turn, are thought to represent the internalized prohibitions of the child's parents (or parent substitutes). The term "instinctual drives" refers to motivations and desires which are basic to human nature, which are powerful, and which are *not altogether to be denied* (7).

Areas of Conflict

Conflict between people is natural, and ubiquitous. It is not a priori unresolvable. In fact, most conflicts are capable of solution to the satisfaction of both parties; and it is only when a solution cannot be found that both parties to the dispute are apt to suffer, in the near or the long term. This is true even when conflicts spring up between relatively unequal parties, such as between a child and his parents.

Psychological development of children (and of adults) tends to proceed by stages or phases (8, 9). At each stage of develop-

---

* Internalization is the process of incorporating or making part of oneself the cultural values, morals, motivations, and conflicts of one's immediate group or culture.

ment the areas of potential conflict between children and their parents are unique, and will never be repeated in quite the same way; that is, they are phase-specific. We will discuss the highlights of the first three phases of development, with particular emphasis on the conflicts to be confronted by parents and child at these times. Briefly stated, these areas of potential conflict center on trust and dependency, aggression, and sexuality.

Dependency and trust. During the first year of life a child is entirely dependent upon his parents for all his bodily and psychological needs. He cannot provide for himself, and everything must be done for him. His need to be ministered to is seemingly unending. For the parents the potential problem exists in accepting the child's dependency as a biological and temporary necessity. What can go wrong is that the parents may resent the child's dependency and be angry with him for something which is not his fault; or they may rather enjoy the all-powerful position they hold in relation to their child and try to keep him in this dependent position far beyond the time when this is necessary or desirable. If the child is basically accepted by his parents, and if they are reasonably consistent in meeting his daily needs, then the child will develop the foundations for a basically trusting attitude toward the world and toward himself. If on the other hand he finds himself unacceptable to his parents, or if they are inconsistent in meeting his needs, frustrating him exceedingly sometimes, indulging him excessively at other times, then he may come to think of himself as not worthwhile and of the world as a hostile place in which one cannot trust other people. The principal anxiety of this period, then, is the fear of abandonment, or the fear of being helplessly at the mercy of another person who is not too kindly disposed.

Aggression. During the second and third year of life the child changes from the dependent and passive infant to the mobile, self-assertive, muscularly co-ordinated toddler. And with this change, the attitude of the parents toward the child may change as well. The child is now beginning to manifest his own will. He learns to run toward mother and away from her, he learns to pick up and move things, turn knobs, open drawers, pick up and throw things; he learns how to say "Mama" and "Daddy" and soon a few sentences as well, and he also learns how to say "No"; he learns to control his bowel movements and to withhold them. This is a period of beginning independence, of open aggression, of of self-assertion, and self-control. Delighted as parents may be with their child's growing skills and independence, they are likely not to be altogether delighted, and of course, some limits to his aggressiveness need to be set. This necessary limit-setting, however, should not be confused with an attitude which either rejects and forbids all manifestation of independence and aggressiveness, or which permits them to go untrammelled. The anxieties of this period are due to a fear of being unacceptable because of one's independent strivings and of one's self-assertive activities.

Sexuality. During the child's next three years of life his development proceeds apace and as it does so it brings with it new areas of possible conflict. The beginnings of sexuality make their first appearance. Along with a growing curiosity about everything in and around themselves, children at this age become interested in their own bodies and the bodies of others. They may discover, accidentally or through mutual exploration, that boys and girls not only dress differently but also are different in certain other respects. They may also discover that there is pleasure to be gained from the manipulation of one's own body, not only in sexual manipulation, but also from running, walking, wrestling, dancing, and other physical contact with others such as hugging or embracing. Spurred by their newly won strengths and abilities, children at this age for the first time begin to imagine being an adult, being like father or like mother, being married to either father or mother. Again, much depends on how the parents respond to these activities and explorations of the children. Ideally, they will accept them in a general way but at the same time provide the child information about social appropriateness. But if the parents respond to every instance of pleasurable bodily activity or sexual curiosity with horrified disapproval, then this area of psychological functioning will be demarcated for the child as something evil and unacceptable. Since sexuality, broadly defined as pleasure derived from the use of one's body, is one of the natural instinctual human needs, and as such is not altogether to be denied, the groundwork for future trouble is being laid if sexuality is repressed or rejected. The anxieties of this period then center on the fear of non-acceptance or actual physical punishment because of one's own forbidden sexuality.

The developments we have discussed here represent the cornerstones of personality formation. But development does not stop here. Throughout life, but particularly at other critical stages, such as at adolescence, in young adulthood, in the mature years, and even in old age, further differentiation occurs in the areas of trust or dependency, of assertiveness, and of sexuality. Unresolved conflict in these areas can give rise to neurotic symptomatology.

Neurotic Symptomatology—A Compromise

If the instinctual drives of an individual cannot be freely expressed (subject only to the reasonable limitations which must be imposed in order for a society to function), they will seek expression nevertheless. The neurotic symptom (and by this we mean not only an isolated symptom, such as an irrational fear which seems to intrude upon the individual's personality, but also certain neurotic personality traits which form an integrated part of the personality) is a compromise between powerful impulses seeking expression and equally powerful prohibitions existing in the same person. The neurotic symptom, as Freud pointed out, has meaning. Its exact meaning can be determined only by careful study of the individual's symptoms and personality. Such careful study will reveal that three general classes of meaning exist in virtually all neurotic symptoms: (a) The symptom represents a barrier to the expression of a forbidden wish or impulse; (b) it also represents the expression of or the yielding to that forbidden impulse, in partial or distorted form; (c) finally, it represents a communication about the existing internal conflict (10).

Before going on to a discussion of types of neurotic behavior, let us look at a brief clinical illustration. We have chosen a rather "obvious" instance, that is, one in which it is fairly easy to see what is going on—"easy to see" for an outside observer, that is, not for the patient!

Illustration: A twenty-four-year-old married woman is referred to the psychiatrist by an ear, nose, and throat specialist. Six weeks before she lost her voice to the point where she could not speak above a whisper. She was examined by several doctors, one of whom told her that she had a small growth on her vocal cords; another, that one of her vocal cords was paralyzed; two more had said that there was nothing wrong with her vocal cords and that it must be "her nerves." She was then seen by an ear, nose, and throat specialist who also found nothing wrong physically, but who, on learning that the patient had been emotionally upset recently, felt that perhaps this might be related to her symptom.

When the patient comes to the psychiatrist's office, she is not alone but has her husband with her. It occurs to the psychiatrist that in bringing her husband along, she has perhaps brought along part of her problem. Ordinarily, psychiatrists prefer to talk to their patients alone, at least initially. But in this case the husband seems exceedingly suspicious, and the psychiatrist feels it would be best if the husband stayed in the office. The patient is a very attractive young woman, with raven black hair, strikingly red lips, a red and black dress, and a very good figure. She whispers. She whispers that for the last six weeks she has been unable to talk normally. Asked what she thinks the trouble is, she shrugs her shoulders in an "I don't know" gesture. But the gesture also conveys an "I don't care" attitude. When the psychiatrist asks if she has been under any emotional strain, she vigorously nods her head while her husband simultaneously denies this. The patient then goes on to whisper to the psychiatrist that she has been experiencing conflict with her mother-in-law over who is to do the household chores. She also mentions, quite casually, that she has been married only a short time and that her husband has been previously married. There have been "whispers" in the community, she whispers, that the husband has been seen again with his former wife. As she talks, the psychiatrist has the distinct feeling the patient is speaking in the manner of someone "whispering behind someone's back." The patient says she has been unhappy, but that she has been "unable to say anything about it."

By now the husband has become less suspicious and excuses himself and steps out of the office, leaving the psychiatrist and the patient alone. The first words the patient utters after the door has closed are, "Now I can talk." But she is still whispering. She says that she has been unable to "talk up" to her husband for fear that he would beat her. She says that the marriage has been unsatisfactory sexually and that her husband seems to care more about his mother than he does about her. She also mentions, again quite casually, that for the last six weeks she has been unable to work at her regular job as a telephone operator. She herself sees no connection between her life situation and her inability to speak normally.

This illustration is interesting from several points of view. First, although we know really very little about this patient, some of the meaning of her symptoms can be guessed. She cannot permit herself to talk up to her husband or to her mother-in-law, nor can she openly ask for anything for herself sexually (prohibition of impulse). She will nevertheless talk up to her husband in a distorted way by making it hard for him to understand her, by being unable to contribute to their income, and by forcing him to incur extensive medical expenses (distorted expression of impulse). Lastly, she is using her symptom to communicate to others the conflict she is experiencing (communicative value of the symptom). It should be clear that this is of course not done with conscious awareness on the part of the patient. It is sometimes possible to guess at motivation by observing the effect that the behavior has on the situation.

CLINICAL TYPES OF NEUROTIC BEHAVIOR

Hysterical Neurosis, Hysterical Personality, and Hysterical Life Style

Most psychiatrists seeing the patient we have described would make a diagnosis of *conversion reaction,* the modern version of what was previously called *hysterical neurosis.* The term "conversion reaction" implies that a complaint in the psychological sphere has, through the use of complicated mental mechanisms,* been *converted* into a physical complaint. The new physical complaint expresses symbolically what the person could not express openly and directly. Now we may well ask why it should be necessary for the person to take this circuitous route. Neurotic people are people who have been hurt in their early explorations of one or another area of feelings. They have trusted, and their trust has been betrayed; they have shown a certain amount of aggressiveness, and they have been severely punished for it; or they have indulged in some sexual activity, and they have been made to feel ashamed, or the act has been forbidden to them. In other words, it was *not safe* to trust, to be aggressive, or to indulge in bodily pleasures. "Safety first" has become their primary concern; safety, however, at the expense of flexibility, at the expense of genuine satisfactions. When the road to genuine satisfactions has been blocked, through anxiety or fear, then substitute satisfactions, viz. neurotic symptoms, must be relied upon. Hysterical or conversion symptoms, such as the one we have described, are in this sense typical of neurotic symptoms or neurotic character traits in general.

Conversion reactions, then, consist of bodily symptoms for which no organic cause can be found; symptoms, moreover, which express symbolically an internal conflict. Conversion reactions most frequently take the form of "inabilities"—"I can't move my right arm," "I can't see," "I can't speak," "I can't feel anything in the lower part of my body." More rarely, pain or involuntary movements are also experienced (12).

The mental mechanisms primarily responsible for hysterical symptoms are (a) repression (expulsion from consciousness) of an unacceptable impulse; (b) symbolization (the choice of a symptom which expresses in metaphorical language the conflict

* For an introduction to the mental mechanisms or defense mechanisms, see Anna Freud (11).

which the patient is experiencing); and (c) conversion (conversion of conflictual anxiety or psychological anguish into physical suffering). Not infrequently the development of a physical symptom (even though it is on an emotional basis) results in certain benefits to the patient which were not fully anticipated. Instead of being treated as an emotionally disturbed person the patient may now be treated, at least by some people, as someone who has a physical ailment and as such deserves to be cared for, excused from his usual responsibilities, and treated with sympathy and concern. These so-called secondary gains (the primary gain would be the partial satisfaction of the forbidden impulse) unfortunately constitute a formidable deterrent to overcoming the neurosis, since giving up the neurotic symptom also means giving up the gratifications derived from being sick.

Some of the same mechanisms operative in the production of hysterical or conversion symptoms are also at work in the functioning of personalities which we describe as hysterical. But it should be pointed out that the relationship between conversion reaction and hysterical personality is not one to one. Conversion reactions may occur as isolated symptoms in other psychiatric disorders, and persons with hysterical personalities need never develop conversion symptoms, although they are perhaps prone to do so (13). Hysterical persons are characterized by an impressionistic, overly dramatic, overly impressionable life style (14). Life is lived by them as though it were a series of theatrical productions, of great immediate but little enduring importance. At one moment life may seem to them a gay, colorful panorama, the next a dark abyss of despair, which in turn will give rise to another equally extreme view of the world or of the person's own situation. The attention of the hysterical person is caught by the most glaring, the most dramatic, the most colorful details—and he bases his conclusions on them rather than on the entire situation. He makes up his mind prematurely, having considered only part (the most dramatic part) of the evidence. As a result his knowledge of the world or himself is not terribly accurate, which in turn accounts for the fact that the feelings he expresses, although intense, seem somewhat false and somehow insincere. The hysterical person has a distinct preference for words that are highly charged emotionally—terrific, great, monstrous, wild, horrible, zowie, wham-bang—rather than for more accurate and less highly charged ones. In fact he communicates much less with words than he does with gestures and bodily movements. But even these may not convey the messages he intends to send or at least the ones he consciously intends to send. We have been speaking thus far of the hysterical person as "he." More often, however, hysterical persons are women. To date we have no good understanding of the affinity of this particular form of personality disturbance for the female sex.

As with conversion reactions, repression, particularly repression of sexual impulses, seems to be the principal defense mechanism in hysterical persons. Symbolization (for instance, many of the utterances or gestures of hysterical persons seem symbolically to allude to sexual matters) is also prominently at work. Hysterical behavior serves the same three compromise functions we have ascribed to all neurotic symptomatology.

Obsessive-Compulsive Neurosis, Compulsive Personality, and Compulsive Style

In many ways compulsive persons are the direct opposites of hysterical persons. Instead of impressionistic, they are precise; instead of dramatic, they are controlled; instead of pliable, they are rigid in their opinions and attitudes. Instead of being distractible, they adhere strictly to plans and schedules. They communicate primarily through words, rather than through bodily expression of feelings; and their choice of words is exact, abstract, unimbued by feelings, and to some degree, dull. While hysterical persons reach premature conclusions, compulsive people prefer never to make a decision or a commitment. They are plagued by doubts to an extreme degree. They always see both the advantages and disadvantages of any given situation, and, as a result, may be completely unable to arrive at a choice between alternatives. As soon as they *have* made a decision, they immediately begin to worry that they have made the wrong one. They are devoted to details, important ones as well as unimportant ones. Continuity and sameness are valued, while novelty and change are shunned. Play and recreation have only minor roles in their lives, while productivity and work dominate. For compulsive people, self-esteem depends almost entirely on what they accomplish, not on what they are or what they feel. Compulsive people are methodical, humorless, and cold. They have been aptly described as living machines.

Compulsiveness, like any other personality trait, is of course, a matter of degree. Mild compulsiveness can actually be an asset in certain jobs or professions, such as in accounting, the practice of medicine, or in other scientific work requiring close attention to detail. But beyond a certain degree, it becomes distinctly disruptive, hampering first quality and enjoyment of work, ultimately reducing quantity of work as well.

Compulsive behavior may be so well integrated into the personality as to constitute a life style (14). We refer to such behavior as ego-syntonic. The patient may say of it: "That's me. That's just the way I am." On the other hand, obsessions and compulsions may also intrude upon the personality as relatively isolated symptoms, and then be regarded as ego-alien. The person may say: "I'm not really like that, but I can't help myself."

Obsessions are unwanted thoughts which intrude, repeatedly and insistently, upon a person's consciousness and which cannot be put aside by the exercise of will power. Obsessional thoughts are generally irrelevant, silly, obscene, or in some other way inappropriate. For instance, every time one patient heard the phone ring, the thought: "something has happened to my father" intruded. Another patient thought, over and over again: "God and the Virgin Mary are lovers." Still another patient had the recurrent thought: "I could kill." None of these thoughts were connected with the feelings appropriate to them. For example, the person who thought, "I could kill," was not aware of any feelings of anger toward anyone.

Compulsions are obligatory acts which the person finds himself carrying out, much against his will and better judgment. But if he tries to abstain from or is in some way prevented from carrying out these acts, he develops severe anxiety which can be relieved only by his giving in to the compulsion. Typical compulsions are: repeated checking to make sure that a door has been locked, touching a series of objects or body parts in a certain ritualistic order, or repeatedly washing one's hands. Sometimes obsessive thoughts are combined with compulsive acts. For instance, one patient had the recurrent thought: "China will start nuclear war." Immediately afterwards he had to wipe his forehead, as if trying to wipe away the thought.

As can be seen, this is indeed strange behavior. What does it signify and how does it come about? The basic motivation for compulsive behavior is the *control of unacceptable instinctual impulses,* particularly of sexual and aggressive impulses. Actually, strong feelings of any kind are unacceptable to such persons, since they imply potential loss of control over feelings. The compromise arrived at in compulsive behavior is that sexual and aggressive impulses can be admitted to consciousness only as isolated thoughts which have been stripped of all feeling content. The extensive rituals and rules which govern the lives of compulsive people are similarly designed to prevent any unforseen outbreak of feelings. So long as no irrevocable decisions have been made, so long as situations are stable and unchanged, the compulsive person feels safe and secure. Asked how he feels, he might reply: "Everything is under control."

Phobic Reactions and Phobic Style

Phobic reactions are the result of another kind of attempt to control unwanted feelings, an attempt which, too, is only partially successful. Certain kinds of feelings are indeed kept out of consciousness while certain others intrude, intermittently and very forcefully, on the personality. Phobias are irrational fears of objects or situations, or of whole classes of objects or situations. Typically, the afflicted person develops a massive outbreak of anxiety when faced with the kind of situation he has learned to fear. He may become completely frozen into panicked immobility, or he may take flight from the situation as though the very devil were after him. It may take several hours before he is calm again, but then he usually functions normally until the next time the same situation is encountered. The phobic person, in trying to cope with his problem, will try to avoid the feared situation. But when this is done, often the fear spreads (generalizes) to include situations only remotely (though definitely and understandably) connected with the original feared stimulus. A few of the typical feared objects or situations are: open spaces, closed spaces, heights, darkness, certain animals, or riding in cars, trains, or airplanes. We can see that all of these situations have some minor potential for danger; but the response accorded them by phobic individuals is clearly excessive.

Phobias are very common in childhood, especially during the pre-school years. (Freud's first published psychoanalytic study of a phobia was of a five-year-old boy (15).) Most childhood phobias are short-lived; they require no psychiatric intervention and tend to disappear spontaneously. While some phobias in adults also disappear spontaneously, this is by no means the rule. Phobias in adults can be very resistant to treatment.

While phobias are generally more or less isolated symptoms impinging on an otherwise well-functioning personality, we also see some persons who have developed a phobic life style. These are people who are generally fearful; they approach all situations with timidity and dread, and they show very little self-assertion. Anything new or strange is regarded by them as dangerous, and hence, as a thing to be avoided. As a result, they lead very narrow lives, confined by their self-inflicted restrictions.

This leads us to inquire into the motivations and mechanisms of phobic behavior. There are two widely held formulations. The first of these, the psychoanalytic one, postulates that phobic behavior develops as a defense against becoming aware of the actual causes of one's anxiety, that is, becoming aware of one's own forbidden competitive, aggressive, or loving impulses. The actual fears cannot be acknowledged and they are therefore displaced onto some neutral object which nevertheless has some symbolic connection with the forbidden impulse.

A second formulation, based on work with conditioning experiments, postulates that phobias are accidentally learned responses; that they represent conditioned responses to adventitious elements of a once actually frightening situation. For instance, if someone was nearly run over by a yellow Mack truck, he may henceforth be afraid of all objects which move and are yellow. Simple and attractive as this explanation may seem, it does not adequately explain why such a response should not in time die out. What the two formulations hold in common is that a mere understanding of the underlying motivation is not enough to overcome the phobia. The patient must also be re-exposed to the feared situation, in graduated doses. He must unlearn his fear, he must be deconditioned (see Chapter 10 on psychotherapy in this book).

Anxiety Reactions

Closely related to the phobic reactions are anxiety reactions. Here the anxiety is not so well focused as in phobias, although the underlying causes are probably similar. The anxiety occurs as so-called free-floating anxiety—the individual is not at all sure why he is anxious. Anxiety may fluctuate in intensity over time, but these fluctuations are never so pronounced as in phobic conditions. The term "anxiety reaction" is somewhat of a wastebasket term. It categorizes anxiety that is not clearly part of other recognizable psychiatric disorders. It may have been surmised already that there are few patterns of disordered behavior that are not characterized by at least the occasional presence of overt anxiety.

Passive-Aggressive Personality

Passive-aggressive behavior is, as the name implies, a compromise between the desire to be aggressive and a strong prohibition against aggressiveness. The result is behavior which on the surface is passive and compliant but which nevertheless has the effect of an attack and often is responded to as though it were an attack. Passive obstructionism is one example. Promising to do an unpleasant task, but "forgetting" to carry it out, is another. Passive-aggressive persons are not in the habit of expressing anger overtly and hence have little experience with expressing anger in small doses; they can become quite dangerous on those few occasions when they do permit themselves to become angry. This usually happens "only in response to repeated provocation" (which they themselves have unconsciously encouraged); they may injure themselves or others or smash up a car or destroy a whole room of furniture. Except for their difficulties in handling aggression, these people lead otherwise relatively satisfying lives.

Schizoid Personality

Schizoid persons are persons who have withdrawn, to a greater or lesser extent, from interaction with other people. Presumably they found early in life that contact with other people was for them severely distressing. As far as is possible they avoid contact with others. These are people who have few or no friends, sometimes become hermits, or earn a living in solitary jobs. These persons should not be confused with schizophrenic persons, although from their number may come a few of those who ultimately develop schizophrenic reactions.

Impulsive Style and Impulsive Personality, Including
Sociopathic Personality

Thus far we have been discussing neurotic behavior which has been the product of internal conflict and characterized by an excessive inhibition of certain instinctual impulses and drives. We now come to a consideration of personality problems which represent, at least superficially, the direct opposite. With impulsive persons, conflicts are not so much internal as they are conflicts between individuals and society, and their impulses, instead of being too well controlled, are not controlled well enough. First let us describe these patterns of behavior. Afterwards we will go on to see if they do not after all have something in common motivationally with those neurotic disorders already discussed.

Excellent descriptions of impulsive or sociopathic persons exist, in literature and in psychiatric writings. Mann's fictional *Confessions of Felix Krull, Confidence Man* and Cleckley's clinical study, *The Mask of Sanity,* provide good starting points (16, 17). Shapiro in his *Neurotic Styles* has formally delineated the characteristics of impulsive style (14). Helpful as these works are, they still do not tell us enough to allow us to form a sound motivational understanding of sociopathic behavior. From them we do learn, however, why such an understanding is difficult to achieve: impulsive persons rarely stand still long enough to afford others a close look into the inner workings of their personality.

Impulsive persons do not stand still for long. They move from place to place, from job to job, from "relationship" to "relationship" without ever establishing any real relationships or ties. They rarely have long-term commitments or goals. They are people of action who live for the moment, not for the future. They have a perfectly adequate understanding of conventional morals and ethics, but they are not bound by them. An impulse strikes them and they immediately carry it into action, whether the impulse be to go off on a trip, to steal some money, to write a false check, to get a job, to marry someone they have just met; whether this be to acquire a college education or to go on a drunk. Little time is wasted in considering the consequences of their actions, and the activities which they have begun can be abandoned as easily as they were started. This makes for a varied and perhaps exciting life, but for a disrupted, discontinuous life as well. The stable trends and themes which are discernible in most of our personalities and our lives are absent from theirs.

Certain personality functions are highly developed in impulsive and sociopathic persons: the ability to quickly "size up" a situation for the possibilities of its providing an immediate advantage; the ability to use words smoothly and glibly to turn such a potential into an actual advantage; the ability to portray whatever feelings seem to be called for to promote their own cause. The fact that these words or "feelings" have no connection with actual facts does not trouble them; it is part of the game. It is a paradox, then, that their great skill in promoting their own welfare, should net them so little in the long run. Their selfish, self-serving, inconsiderate, and sometimes cruel behavior with other people is in the long run self-damaging and self-defeating. Their meteoric rises (in business dealings, in the stock market, in their "friendships" with important personages) are always followed by nose-dive falls. For them, nothing lasts. For instance, a man may stage a daring bank robbery and get away without being identified or caught. He immediately starts to spend money lavishly so as to attract the attention of the police. Or another man may charm a beautiful and desirable woman into promising to marry him, but as soon as he has her promise he manages to let her find out that he has simultaneously proposed marriage to her best friend. And so on, and so on.

We have made no particular distinction between impulsive and sociopathic persons (18). The term "sociopathic" implies that a person's impulsiveness is principally directed against society, and that he has repeatedly come into conflict with its written and unwritten laws. It also implies that he has no conscience, never experiences guilt, remorse, or anxiety, and that he is never really sincere. This is probably not altogether true. Such persons do at times express feelings of guilt, remorse, and anxiety, but with them these feelings are of a very fleeting nature, and hence appear to us as false or as shams. But we have also encountered this apparent falseness of feelings in other types of neurotic behavior, for instance, in hysterical behavior. If it had meaning there, we should also look for its underlying meaning in sociopathic behavior.

If one is able to get an impulsive (or sociopathic) person to hold still long enough (and this can usually be done only in prison where the person has no choice about remaining or leaving), one will gradually discover that he is a person who as a child was extremely deprived—of affection, of consistent limit-setting, of consistent parental figures with whom he could identify and whose code of morals and ethics he could adopt. Very early in life he learned to relate to other people through cunning, not through trust. He learned that the way to get something from others was to manipulate them into giving. As one becomes still better acquainted with the impulsive person one discovers in him a tremendous reservoir of depression and an overwhelming feeling that he has been unloved and unlovable. Still later in such a relationship one may see the impulsive person reach out, very tentatively, toward the other person, all the time expecting to be rejected or betrayed. In other words, one finally does come upon a deeply buried internal conflict. The conflict here is one of wanting to trust, of wanting to commit oneself lovingly to another person, yet being afraid of betrayal, fearful that the effort will not be rewarded.

The possible varieties of neurotic experience have not been exhausted by this presentation. They are, in fact, endless. What we have done is to devote the space available to some general features of neurotic behavior in the belief that light will be shed on neurotic behavior, in whatever form it may be encountered.

References

1. Otto Fenichel, *The Psychoanalytic Theory of the Neuroses*, Norton, New York, 1945.
2. Harry S. Sullivan, *Conceptions of Modern Psychiatry*, William A. White Psychiatric Foundation, Washington, D.C., 1947.
3. George Engel, *Psychological Development in Health and Disease*, Saunders, Philadelphia, 1962.
4. Heinz Hartmann, *Ego Psychology and the Problem of Adaptation*, International Universities Press, New York, 1958.
5. Harry S. Sullivan, *The Interpersonal Theory of Psychiatry*, Norton, New York, 1953.
6. George Engel, "Anxiety and Depression-Withdrawal: The Primary Affects of Unpleasure," *Int. J. Psycho-analysis*, 43:89–97, 1962.
7. Frederick R. Hine, personal communication.
8. Erik H. Erikson, *Childhood and Society*, second edition, Norton, New York, 1963.
9. Erik H. Erikson, *Identity and the Life Cycle*, International Universities Press, New York, 1959.
10. Sigmund Freud, *A General Introduction to Psychoanalysis*, Garden City Publishing Co., Garden City, N.Y., 1938.
11. Anna Freud, *The Ego and the Mechanisms of Defense*, International Universities Press, New York, 1946.
12. J. J. Purtell, E. Robins and M. E. Cohen, "Observations on the Clinical Aspects of Hysteria," *J.A.M.A.*, 146:902–9, 1951.
13. Paul Chodoff, *et al.*, "Hysteria, the Hysterical Personality and Hysterical Conversion," *Amer. J. Psychiat.*, 114:734, 1958.
14. David Shapiro, *Neurotic Styles*, Basic Books, New York, 1965.
15. Sigmund Freud, "The Analysis of a Phobia in a Five-Year-Old Boy," in *Collected Papers*, Vol. III, Hogarth Press, London, 1956.
16. Thomas Mann, *Confessions of Felix Krull*, Knopf, New York, 1946.
17. Hervey M. Cleckley, *The Mask of Sanity*, Mosby, St. Louis, 1964.
18. Joseph J. Michaels, "Character Structure and Character Disorders," in S. Arieti, editor, *American Handbook of Psychiatry*, Basic Books, New York, 1959.

6

Suicide

Suicide is the intentional, sometimes violent, taking of one's own life. Its impact on those who remain behind is far greater than that of death from any other cause, evoking shock, bewilderment, and consternation. It produces, among relatives and friends of the deceased, feelings of guilt, shame, anger, and doubt. Death from physical disease, on the other hand, is more easily understood and accepted. But it is difficult, for professional and layman alike, to face the admission that a person died deliberately, by his own hand, and the question is often asked, "How was it possible for this to happen?" Answers to this question do not come easily. What is clear is that suicide does happen, and not infrequently.

Suicide springs from hopelessness and despair (1). For this reason it is of interest to the psychiatrist. But it is of course a matter of concern to other physicians as well, and to all citizens generally. Each year large numbers of people commit suicide. That is to say, they die unnecessarily; for suicide is preventable; it is not inevitable.

Actual Suicide vs. Attempted Suicide

In order to understand the problems of suicide and of suicide prevention we must focus not only on persons who have actually committed suicide, but also on those who contemplate, threaten, or unsuccessfully try to commit suicide. For out of their number will come those who actually kill themselves. Persons who actually commit suicide have, as a group, rather different characteristics from those who attempt suicide and fail. One obvious difference between the two groups is that people who successfully commit suicide are no longer available for either treatment or study, while those who fail remain with us, challenging us to understand their actions and to help them cope with life's problems. Other differences will be discussed below.

Actual Suicide—Statistics

Each year some 20,000 persons in the United States take their own lives. Though the figure varies somewhat from year to year, the total number is always formidable. In 1964 (the latest year for which complete statistics are available), when 191,371,000 persons were living in the United States, 20,588 persons committed suicide (2). This amounts to an annual rate of 10.8 per 100,000 persons. Rates vary in different countries, ranging from a low of 2.5 per 100,000 in Ireland to a rate of 30.0 per 100,000 in West Germany (3). In the United States, certain sections of the country report higher rates; for example in Los Angeles County the annual rate is 14.5 per 100,000 population (4). Monroe County, in upstate New York, where a psychiatric case register supplements the records of the county medical examiner, the annual rate of suicide is 9.7 per 100,000 population, or very close to the national average (5). Such figures must be recognized as minimal, for not all suicidal deaths are recognized as such (some look or are made to look like accidents), and not all recognized suicides are so recorded.

Suicide ranks high among the leading causes of death. Over-all, it is the eleventh leading cause of death (among male Caucasians it ranks eighth). In some states it is sixth, and among college students and peacetime soldiers it ranks third, behind malignant neoplasms and accidents (6).

The rate of actual suicide increases dramatically with age, but the increase with age is particularly impressive for men. The suicide rate for men age 20–24 is 10 per 100,000. In the age group 40 to 55 it has risen to 25 per 100,000, and at age 80 it has reached 60 per 100,000, six times that of the population as a whole. For women the rate of suicide is about 5 per 100,000 at age 20 to 24; it rises to about 10 per 100,000 by middle age, and thereafter remains about level for the remainder of the life span. Over-all, three times as many men commit suicide as women—during 1964, in the United States, 15,092 men and 5496 women committed suicide.

It is tempting to speculate why suicide rates increase with age and why they are higher among men, but no undisputed data exist to answer these questions. Two suggestions do seem to have some merit, however: that fewer and fewer hopes remain as age advances; and that men in our society are emotionally less well protected than women. These questions obviously deserve further study.

Suicide Attempts—Statistics

The number of persons who attempt suicide is many times that of those who actually commit suicide. In Monroe County, New York, which we have already mentioned, suicide attempts outnumber actual suicides 3.5 to 1. In Los Angeles County the ratio of attempted to completed suicides is 8 to 1. According to Dublin, using statistics of the Metropolitan Life Insurance Company, in the entire United States the ratio is 7 to 1 (13). It is interesting to note that while three times as many men commit suicide as women, many more women make unsuccessful suicide attempts than men.

We have mentioned that statistics on actual suicides are not complete and probably underestimate their frequency. Of suicide attempts this is true to an even greater degree, largely because many persons who attempt suicide are never seen by physicians or by the police, who might keep such statistics. Even where doctors' and police records are kept, these are not necessarily complete or accurate. This is especially so in cases where the suicidal effort is an obvious attempt at manipulating the environment. This last point brings us to a more general consideration of why people make suicidal efforts at all.

PSYCHOLOGICAL AND SOCIAL ASPECTS OF SUICIDE

We do not know why some persons wish to end their lives. That is, we do not know exactly. Students of human behavior have been both intrigued and concerned with this question, and certain interesting and helpful theories have emerged. Thus, Freud felt that the dynamics of suicide were an extension of the dynamics of depression which we have previously defined as a pathological response to an object loss. Freud further believed that suicide could occur only when an individual, having experienced the loss of an object, incorporated the object into his own ego, and then proceeded to express his hostility toward the lost object by using the self as object and destroying it (7). Menninger enlarged upon this theory, keeping the aggressive elements of the act in the foreground. He held that for suicide to occur three motives were necessary: the wish to kill; the wish to be killed; the wish to die (8). It would appear from clinical data that the aggressive motivations play a greater role with the younger person who commits suicide, while the wish to die, to withdraw, assumes greater importance with an older person.

Psychiatric Diagnosis of Persons Actually Committing Suicide

Are persons who actually commit suicide psychiatrically ill? Based on several studies, the answer to this question must be: "For the most part, yes." Robins evaluated the histories of 134 successful suicides by means of systematic interviews with their relatives, friends, physicians, and clergymen. He found that 94 per cent of the group had been psychiatrically ill, while an additional 4 per cent had had a terminal medical illness. Only 2 per cent had been "apparently clinically well." He further found that two diagnostic categories contributed most to the group of actual suicides: patients with depressive psychoses (45 per cent) and patients with chronic alcoholism (23 per cent); patients with chronic organic brain disease accounted for 4 per cent, constituting the next highest diagnostic category (9). Gardner has reported comparable findings, pointing again to the high risk of suicide among depressed older men and among chronic alcoholics. His work has singled out one additional diagnostic category with very high suicide risk: young male paranoid schizophrenic patients (3). Thus we see that there is a preponderance of psychotic disorders among those who commit suicide.

Psychiatric Diagnosis of Persons Attempting Suicide

Among those who merely attempt suicide the diagnoses are much more varied. Included are a few with psychotic disorders, but the majority consists of persons with neurotic, characterological, and situational problems (10). This leads us to ask whether these persons actually wish to die, or whether their act is designed to accomplish something else.

The Wish To Be Rescued

Jenson, who studied in depth a group of patients who attempted suicide but who did not die, found that in them the "wish to be rescued" formed a major part of their motivation for the attempt (11). They saw the attempt as a magical action which would bring about a solution to their problems. They had the expectation that someone, usually a specific person in their environment, would recognize their plight and take definitive action to improve their situation. Farberow and Shneidman have similarly pointed out that a suicide attempt often constitutes a "cry for help" (12).

There are distinct dangers in this method of seeking help. On the one hand the person may not be rescued and may die. On the other hand the person may be rescued, but his life situation is not improved, and attempted suicide may be followed by actual suicide.

Lethal Probability

Weiss, on the basis of his clinical studies, has pointed out that persons who attempt suicide do not form a homogeneous group. He has described a continuum of lethal probability, high, low, and intermediate (13).

High lethal probability refers to persons who fully intend to take their lives, who definitely expect to die as a result of their action, but who are saved through ignorance of methods, a chance occurrence, or medical intervention. This group probably represents no more than 20 per cent of those who attempt suicide.

Low lethal probability refers to persons who fully intend *not* to die, but who are trying to effect some change in persons or situations significant to them. In most such attempts the methods used will not result in serious harm, or they will be carried out under circumstances in which rescue is certain. Again, such persons probably constitute no more than 20 per cent of those who attempt suicide.

Intermediate lethal probability is the category claiming the greatest number of persons who attempt suicide. These are persons who are uncertain (ambivalent) about whether to live or to die. They would like to live if certain things within themselves or within the environment could be changed for the better, but not if they are to remain the same or grow worse. Their methods of attempting suicide often reflect this ambivalence. They choose methods that have some chance but no certainty of resulting in death. And their provisions for rescue, arrived at consciously or unconsciously, are similarly not foolproof. These persons truly gamble with death, leaving the outcome of their attempt in the hands of significant others or to fate.

There is reason to believe that those persons who actually succeed are guided by somewhat different motives than those who attempt suicide and fail. Certainly we must be more cautious in expressing the probable motives for suicide among those who complete the act. Even where such patients have been under psychiatric or psychoanalytic study prior to their deaths, we cannot be certain that other circumstances and other motives did not play a role at the time they actually carried out the act. The reasons (motives, etiology, causes) for suicide remain an enigma, and a challenge for further research.

SUICIDE ATTEMPTS IN OLDER PERSONS

Persons beyond age sixty who attempt suicide (but who do not die from the attempt) represent a special problem. The intentions behind such attempts must be recognized as being a great deal more serious than in unsuccessful attempts by younger persons. One study, in fact, has shown that both in terms of psychiatric diagnoses as well as in terms of sex distribution, they resemble closely the group of people who actually commit suicide: that is, they are either seriously depressed, alcoholic, or suffer from chronic brain disease; as with actual suicides the men in the group outnumber the women three to one (14). Batchelor in England and Gardner in this country have reported similar findings (15, 3). Gardner in particular has drawn attention to a singularly lethal constellation of psychological and social factors. Suicide is most likely to occur among older men who become depressed, who are chronically addicted to alcohol, and who live alone, in rooming houses and small hotels, in deteriorating center sections of cities. Gardner points out that they are persons who are in the highest risk category for suicide; at the same time they have the lowest likelihood of being seen by a physician or by helping agencies.

Evaluation of the Gravity of Suicidal Risk

We have indicated that not all persons who threaten or attempt suicide are equally serious in their intent. As a first step in the treatment of such persons it is necessary to assess the risk of their actually committing suicide. This is a demanding task. It first requires knowledge of some of the factors which, if present, make actual suicide statistically either more or less probable. Findings that favor a fatal outcome are: the person is male; he is middle-aged or older; he is psychotically depressed or he is an alcoholic; he lives alone; he has no job; he is not trying to bring anyone to terms nor is he expecting that his action will improve his life situation; he has used or is considering using shooting, hanging, or drowning as a method of suicide. Findings that favor a non-fatal outcome are: the person is female; she is young; her distress is related to an acute life crisis; she is trying to influence the behavior of someone close to her; she has used or is considering using low doses of aspirin or sleeping pills or superficial wrist cutting as a method of suicide; the person against whom the attempt or threat was directed has already begun to respond in the desired manner.

These factors are all relatively clear-cut, and their presence or absence is fairly easily determined. Unfortunately only a small portion of suicidal patients fall into these extreme categories of very high or very low risk. In the majority of patients we find signs pointing in both directions. We must then search for additional clues, some of them extremely subtle, in order to arrive at a valid assessment of risk. For instance, the fact that a person openly speaks of wanting to commit suicide is no guarantee that he will not do so; Robins and his co-workers found that the majority of persons who actually committed suicide did, in the days and weeks preceding their deaths, communicate their intention to one or more persons (16). Neither can we assume that someone who has just (unsuccessfully) attempted suicide and who is now saying that he "didn't really mean it" is necessarily revealing his true intentions. He may be, or he may be hiding his actual intentions in order to carry out the act successfully the next time an opportunity presents itself. How are we to know?

We cannot know with absolute certainty. But we can be alert to *incongruities in the patient's behavior* which might tip the balance of our judgment one way or another: incongruities between how the patient says he feels and how others describe his behavior; between how he says he feels and how we, as interacting observers, think he feels, as judged by the feelings he induces in us; between his reported behavior at the time of the suicide attempt and his explanation of that behavior at the time of the evaluation. For instance, a young man who had been found wandering back and forth on a bridge was brought to the hospital emergency room by the police. He told the examining psychiatrist that he had planned to take his life because he had failed a college examination; that now he had changed his mind, however, and wanted to live. He said he was grateful to the police for finding him and he thanked the examining psychiatrist elaborately for "all that you have done for me" and readied himself to leave. The psychiatrist realized that nothing had actually been accomplished and that the man's situation had not changed; he therefore asked him to stay in the hospital for further observation. Later the man confided that if he had been permitted to go home, he would have gotten his father's revolver and shot himself. In another instance a woman was brought to the emergency room after she had been hit by a moving bus. She was only slightly injured, but the bus driver reported that he thought she had deliberately stepped into the path of the bus. The woman denied this, saying it was an accident. Since she showed no obvious signs of emotional disturbance, the doctor who had examined her (a surgeon) permitted her to go home. When her husband came to pick her up he casually mentioned to the doctor that his wife had recently been inquiring about procedures for donating one's body to medical research. The doctor became concerned and asked for an immediate psychiatric consultation. Confronted with the psychiatrist the woman broke down crying, saying that she felt she had needed psychiatric help for a long time. She also admitted that she had intended to kill herself by walking in front of the bus.

TREATMENT OF SUICIDAL PATIENTS

When a person attempts or threatens suicide he is thereby demonstrating extreme distress, and intervention of some kind is generally indicated. Its nature will depend on an assessment of the seriousness of suicidal intent and of the underlying causes for it. When suicidal risk is thought to be great, immediate hospitalization affords the best protection for the patient. Many suicidal patients accept hospitalization readily.* It should be pointed out, however, that the law in most states also authorizes involuntary hospitalization of suicidal patients. When there is significant doubt about the necessity for hospital protection, it is best to err on the side of safety.

Hospitalization, of course, is only one form of intervention and is reserved for those most seriously in danger of taking their own lives. Many other, less drastic remedial measures are possible. Often a brief interview with a psychiatrist is helpful. It can establish for the patient that a crisis exists, what the nature of the crisis is, and what possible courses of action are available to him. It can also lead to the initiation of on-going psychotherapy, of vocational or marriage counselling, of social or welfare assistance, of essential medical care or legal aid, depending of course on the specific needs of the distressed individual. Generally it is not enough to merely advise the patient that he should seek this or that form of help. He must be put in direct contact with the proposed helping agent, whether this be a relative, a friend, the patient's employer, or a staff member of a community service

* It is interesting that even though a person may be seeking death in all earnestness, he may nevertheless accept hospitalization willingly, thereby indicating that he is not entirely of one mind about wanting to die.

agency. Moreover, the psychiatrist must remain in the picture until the helping agent has offered some concrete assistance and the patient has accepted that assistance as meaningful to him. Failing this, the psychiatrist must of necessity fill the breach himself. A few examples can illustrate how this principle of *re-establishing meaningful involvement* can be applied in diverse suicidal crisis situations.

A girl of twenty had swallowed a bottle of sleeping pills in response to her boyfriend's breaking off with her. Her roommate had found her in a slightly drowsy state and brought her to the hospital. The girl readily admitted what she had done but insisted that her boyfriend not be told about what had happened. A little later she volunteered his phone number, "if you really must call him." The boyfriend was in fact called and hurriedly came to the hospital. He felt guilty and very upset over what had happened and said that he would never have left the girl if he had known that he meant so much to her. While obviously there were problems in this interaction which might need to be dealt with therapeutically at some future time, it was equally clear that the acute suicidal crisis was now over.

A more complex case was that of a woman in her middle forties who was brought to a metropolitan hospital by neighbors after they had noticed the smell of cooking gas coming from her apartment. The woman said that she had intended to kill herself because she had nowhere to turn. She told of having recently come to the city from the coal mining part of the state because her husband had developed a lung ailment and could no longer work in the mines. The couple had hoped he might find lighter work in the city. Shortly after they came to the city the husband died suddenly. Their modest savings went for the cost of the funeral. Afterwards the woman tried to find work herself. After weeks of making the rounds of employment offices she was still without a job. She was now completely without funds and without hope. At this point she decided to commit suicide. This woman did not suffer from any major psychiatric disturbance but had been overwhelmed by a series of unfortunate circumstances. To hospitalize her would have been inappropriate. The examining psychiatrist instead referred her to a social worker who was willing to help her get back on her feet. The social worker first allowed the woman to talk freely about the events of the last few weeks and then reflected that the woman's discouragement was certainly understandable, but that it was now time to take positive steps to improve her life circumstances. She explained the availability of temporary financial assistance, took the woman to a welfare office and afterwards to the state employment agency where she helped her fill out a job application. She then returned the woman to her apartment and asked one of the neighbors to spend the evening with her, having made an appointment to see her the next day. The social worker made sure that the woman knew how to get to her office and that she had sufficient bus fare. She appeared the next morning, ten minutes early and considerably brightened in spirits. Together they considered the advantages and drawbacks of returning to her home town and of remaining in the city. The woman decided that she would remain. A few days later she was offered a job as a stock clerk in a department store and accepted it. She returned to see the social worker several more times, but gradually made friends at work and where she lived and was well on her way to establishing herself in her new community. In this case it would not have been sufficient to simply advise her to find employment and to seek temporary financial assistance. She literally had to be shown what to do by the social worker who stood by until no longer needed.

In another instance, a woman in her thirties with chronic medical problems which included arthritis, kidney disease, and some glandular abnormalities, was interviewed following a suicide attempt. She had had numerous psychiatric hospitalizations for severe depression and had previously attempted suicide. She was married but her relationship with her husband was extremely unsatisfactory. She complained that nothing had been done for her medically, that nothing could be done, and that she simply wanted to die. The psychiatrist who took on her care realized that he was dealing with someone with chronic problems and also realized that this woman was, apart from her involvement in her medical care, not involved with anyone else in her personal life or in the community. He virtually forced her into developing a relationship with him by saying that he would not permit her to die and that he would help her over her current depression. He also told her that he could understand that she might from time to time become depressed again but if she ever was in danger of losing control over her suicidal impulse, she must call the psychiatrist. She replied that this was of course ridiculous because if she really felt like killing herself she certainly would not call him. The doctor insisted that she must call him even if it were after she had already taken something which might be harmful to her. He saw her over a period of years in regular psychothera-peutic sessions in which he discussed her day-to-day problems. He learned from her that she was a good gardener and asked her from time to time to bring in some house plants for his office. He also learned that she was a good cook and he accepted several delicious cakes from her. She became severely depressed on many occasions, and twice she took overdoses of sleeping pills but im-mediately afterwards called the doctor, telling him what she had done. Relatively few patients require this kind of intensive reach-ing out described here, but where it is necessary the effort can prove life-preserving.

There is no single, foolproof way of treating suicidal patients. The problems leading up to suicidal efforts are manifold, and the personalities of individuals with such problems are diverse. The therapeutic approaches must be varied accordingly. One factor, however, seems to be central to the prevention of suicide. In order to be saved from his own destructive impulses the patient must be *meaningfully involved* with at least one or more persons in his environment.

A number of *suicide rescue centers* which are based on this principle of meaningful engagement have been set up in large metropolitan areas. These centers operate on an around-the-clock basis and are geared to respond to persons who for one or another reason want to take their own lives but who chose to ask for help at the last moment. The most active of these centers in the United States are the Suicide Rescue Center, in Los Angeles; Rescue, Inc., in Boston; National Save-a-Life Leagues in New York City; and FRIENDS, in Miami. Around the country, many hospital emergency departments provide a similar resource point for persons who have temporarily given up hope.

REFERENCES

1. Leston L. Havens, "Recognition of Suicidal Risks through the Psychological Examination," *New England J. Med.*, 276:210, 1967.
2. U. S. Bureau of the Census, *Statistical Abstracts of the United States: 1966* (87th Edition), Washington, D. C., 1966.
3. Louis I. Dublin, *Suicide*, Ronald Press, New York, 1963.
4. Edwin S. Shneidman and Norman L. Farberow, *Clues to Suicide*, McGraw-Hill, New York, 1957.
5. E. A. Gardner, A. K. Bahn and M. Mack, "Suicide and Psychiatric Care in the Aging," *Arch. Gen. Psychiat.*, 10:547–53, 1964.
6. Edwin S. Shneidman and Norman L. Farberow, "Suicide—The Problem and Its Magnitude," U. S. Veterans' Administration, Department of Medicine and Surgery, Medical Bulletin, MB-7, 1961.
7. Sigmund Freud, "Mourning and Melancholia," in *Collected Papers*, Vol. IV, Hogarth Press, London, 1925.
8. Karl Menninger, *Man Against Himself*, Harcourt, Brace, New York, 1938.
9. E. Robins, G. E. Murphy, R. H. Wilkinson, Jr., S. Gassner and J. Kayes, "Some Clinical Considerations in the Prevention of Suicide Based on a Study of 134 Successful Suicides," *Amer. J. Public Health*, 49:888–99, 1959.
10. E. H. Schmidt, P. O'Neal and E. Robins, "Evaluation of Suicide Attempts as Guide to Therapy; Clinical and Follow-up Studies of 109 Patients," *J.A.M.A.*, 155:549–57, 1954.
11. Viggo W. Jenson, *et al.*, "The Fantasy of Being Rescued in Suicide," *Psychoanalytic Quart.*, 27:32–9, 1958.
12. Norman L. Farberow and Edwin S. Shneidman, *The Cry for Help*, McGraw-Hill, New York, 1961.
13. James M. Weiss, "The Gamble with Death and Attempted Suicide," *Psychiatry*, 20:17–25, 1957.
14. P. O'Neal, E. Robins and E. H. Schmidt, "A Psychiatric Study of

Attempted Suicide in Persons Over 60 Years of Age," *A.M.A. Arch. Neurol. & Psychiat.*, 75:275–84, 1956.
15. I. R. C. Batchelor and M. B. Napier, "Attempted Suicide in Old Age," *Brit. Med. J.*, 2:1186, 1953.
16. E. Robins, S. Gassner, J. Kayes, R. H. Wilkinson, Jr., and G. E. Murphy, "The Communication of Suicidal Intent: A Study of 134 Consecutive Cases of Successful (Completed) Suicide," *Amer. J. Psychiat.*, 115:724–33, 1959.

7

Alcoholism and the Addictions

By discussing alcoholism and drug addiction in a common chapter we are making a judgment that the two disorders are related. In what ways they are related will be made clear as we go along; we will also make clear in what important ways they differ. The regard alcoholics and drug addicts have for each other points up an interesting fact: neither wishes to be placed in the same category with the other. Each has a somewhat derogatory but at the same time awesome view of the other. The alcoholic will say, "I'm no dope fiend." The drug addict will say, "I'm no wino."

We recognize that the terms "dope fiend" and "wino" are stereotypes. Stereotypes are based for the most part on regularly recurrent patterns of behavior, but in some cases they arise out of the need to deal comfortably with problems that are highly charged, highly complex, or give rise to a strong conflict. Alcoholism and drug addiction are just such problems. There are other stereotypes of the "typical alcoholic" or the "typical drug addict" and they are honored not only by alcoholics and addicts themselves but by lay persons in general. They are given credence to some degree by health professionals as well. The existence of stereotypes makes objective investigation and treatment of these conditions exceedingly difficult. The problem needing investigation becomes unattractive automatically and unrecognized bias on the part of the investigator may simply result in a confirmation of the existing stereotype.

ALCOHOLISM

DEFINITIONS

Definitions of alcoholism and of the alcoholic abound, indicating that no universally satisfactory definition exists. There are several definitions, however, which are widely quoted and accepted. The World Health Organization has defined alcoholics as "those excessive drinkers whose dependence upon alcohol has attained such a degree that it shows a noticeable mental disturbance or an interference with their bodily and mental health, their inter-personal relations, and their smooth social and economic functioning; or who show the prodromal signs of such developments" (1). Jellinek, the great pioneer in the field of alcoholism, defines alcoholics rather broadly as individuals who abuse alcohol to such an extent that the individual, society, or both, are harmed (2). Alcoholics Anonymous, the nation's leading self-help group for alcoholics, defines them as persons who have lost the ability to control their drinking (3).

Numerous other definitions exist, some narrow and highly technical, some general and overly inclusive. We cannot do justice to all of them here. However, we would like to point out that not one of the generally accepted definitions of alcoholism stipulates a specific amount or a specific frequency of alcohol intake. In fact, criteria of frequency and quantity are most likely to be cited by individuals who wish to prove to themselves or to others that they are *not* alcoholics. For instance, one frequently hears statements like: "I can't be an alcoholic, I only drink on weekends" or "I can't be an alcoholic, I only drink beer." There is one final definition which may be worth mentioning, not because of its sophistication, but because of its common sense: alcoholics are people who drink too much.

Is Alcoholism a Disease?

The question of whether alcoholism is a disease is one to which no satisfactory answer can be given, although it is currently fashionable as well as politic to refer to it as a disease (4). To so label it has several implications. On the one hand this may lead to greater acceptance of alcoholics as suffering persons who need treatment and understanding. It may also be easier for those in the field to obtain financial support for research, treatment, and rehabilitation programs. On the other hand, consideration of alcoholism as a disease may also be misused. For instance, it may be used by alcoholics to disown any responsibility for their condition and thus make treatment and rehabilitation more difficult. More important perhaps is the fact that alcoholism does not meet the usual criteria of a disease in that etiological factors or mechanisms which are both necessary and sufficient have not been identified (5). Of course, excessive drinking continued over a period of years may lead to disease states of a number of organ systems, but this is not a uniform or necessary consequence of alcoholism. We would therefore prefer to think of *alcoholism not as a disease but as an established pattern of disordered behavior which in a certain percentage of individuals can lead to patterns of disordered physiology as well.*

The Extent of the Problem

Alcoholics are recruited from the ranks of those who drink socially. It has been estimated that more than half of the adults in the United States drink alcoholic beverages on a regular basis. Of those who drink, about one in thirteen becomes an alcoholic. Figures compiled for 1956 indicate that there were 4760 alcoholics for every 100,000 adults. The ratio of male to female alcoholics was 5.8 to 1. The estimate of the total number of alcoholics for that year was five million (6). These figures indicate the size of the problem. Our estimate that presently there are some six million alcoholics in the United States is based on a rise in population from 169 million in 1956 to 195 million in 1966 (7).

CAUSES OF ALCOHOLISM

What causes men and women to drink to excess? It would be erroneous to assume that all who do, do so for the same reasons. In truth, we know very little about the actual causes of alcoholism, and it might be more accurate to speak of patterns of development of alcoholism rather than of truly etiological factors. Presumably the differing patterns of development will shed light on differing etiological factors.

Instant Addicts

There are, for example, alcoholics who become addicted to alcohol almost with their first drink. In general, these are individuals (usually young people) who in their ordinary day-to-day living have been unable to achieve anything approaching interpersonal security, having been deprived of rewarding and satisfying interpersonal experiences. No human contacts, nor contacts with nature or the arts, nor any work experience and accomplishment have been able to allay their basic dis-ease, anxieties, and self-doubts. To such persons their first experience with alcohol is a revelation. For the first time they may be free from anxiety and be free to participate in interpersonal relationships to a fuller degree than ever before. More important perhaps, the state of well-being is one which they themselves have induced, independent of the good will of others. Henceforth, when solace is needed, they will seek it in alcohol. Soon this becomes the overriding concern and preoccupation, and alcoholism becomes a firmly established, and grim, fact. Individuals who succumb so quickly to the lure of alcohol make up only a small percentage of alcoholics. Most alcoholics experience a gradual seduction, while the opposite is true of narcotic addicts.

Gradual Seduction

Alcoholism develops most commonly as an outgrowth of a culturally established and culturally approved pattern of social drinking. The transition from controlled to uncontrolled drinking may take from two to twenty years, and usually proceeds by stages or phases which have been well described (see below). But why is it that some people gradually lose control over their drinking behavior while most do not?

Much has been made of the so-called alcoholic personality. Using clinical impressions as our basis, we describe the typical alcoholic as emotionally immature, impulsive, overly dependent, and unable to delay gratifications. The immediate relief from anxiety obtainable through drinking is preferred to the slower and more arduous task of realistic problem solving. While accurate as a description of alcoholic behavior, the concept of the alcoholic personality leaves something to be desired as an explanation. For one thing, objective personality inventories, such as the Minnesota Multiphasic Personality Inventory, do not substantiate the notion of a specific personality profile (8). Rather, alcoholics show many different types of personality patterns. This has led one investigator to remark rather cynically that the only characteristic which alcoholics have in common is the fact that they drink too much (9).

Phases of Gradually Developing Alcoholism

Since gradual development is the most common way in which alcoholism is established, more is known about this mode of development. In particular, the phases of drinking behavior through which an individual passes have been well studied. Basing his notions on the drinking histories of 2000 male alcoholics, Jellinek has given the following account (10):

During the *pre-alcoholic symptomatic phase* the alcoholic-to-be experiences greater pleasure and greater relief from anxiety by drinking in social situations than is usual with most people. This is self-reinforcing and leads to more frequent drinking. With frequent imbibition comes tolerance, that is, increasingly larger quantities of alcohol are required to produce the same effect. Although the individual at this stage may not drink to the point of drunkenness very often, the quantities of alcohol which are being consumed in a given period of time are becoming prodigious.

During the *prodromal phase* several new patterns of behavior make their appearance. Occasional blackouts, or periods of amnesia for the events of a drinking bout, may occur for the first time. Sneaking drinks, or clandestine drinking, develops. Preoccupation with alcohol and craving for alcohol begin. Rapid or avid drinking in the early stages of a drinking bout can be observed. Shame and guilt over the excessive drinking make themselves felt and lead to "covering-up" behavior and still poorly developed rationalizations.

During the *crucial phase* the individual begins to experience a physical need for alcohol. Without it he feels tense, tremulous, generally miserable, and not at all his usual self. He requires a few drinks in the morning to restore his equilibrium. He may even have to lay in a supply of liquor at his job to help him get through the day. At this point his drinking is beginning to interfere materially with his job performance. In fact, he has lost control over his drinking behavior. Realizing this, he tries to regain control by changing his drinking pattern in some way. For instance, he may decide not to drink until after five o'clock, or to drink only wine, or only beer, or not to mix his drinks, or to drink only at home. His entire behavior becomes alcohol-centered. He is pre-occupied with where and when it will be possible for him to drink. Other considerations recede into the background. He is now clearly addicted.

During the *chronic phase* rationalizations fall away and the individual gives himself over to drunkenness. He now allows himself to become intoxicated in the daytime and goes on prolonged "benders." Such behavior leads to marked social disapproval. He may be fired from his job, his wife may leave him, he may run afoul of the law because of public intoxication or disorderly conduct. He has fewer and fewer people to turn to and his self-esteem sinks to a low ebb. At this stage medical complications affecting the central nervous system or other bodily systems (see below) may make their appearance. He may drift towards the skid row section of his community and become a public drunk. He can sink no lower; he has hit "rock bottom." It should be made clear that not all alcoholics reach this last stage; moreover, treatment can be begun as soon as the problem is recognized.

Symptomatic Alcoholism

We have mentioned two ways in which alcoholism can develop. There is a third set of circumstances which can lead to alcoholism. This happens when individuals with one of the major psychiatric disturbances (especially schizophrenia and severe depression) discover, often quite by accident, that sizable quantities of alcohol relieve their symptoms temporarily. The experience may be repeated, at increasingly frequent intervals, using increasingly larger quantities of alcohol as tolerance develops. Soon the individual is both emotionally and physically dependent on alcohol. The basic underlying psychiatric disturbance may go unrecognized, and the patient may be regarded by his family and by his physician as "just another alcoholic." Once the specific psychiatric problem is recognized, however, specific psychiatric treatment may be instituted (see Chapter 3, Schizophrenia, and Chapter 2, Affective Disorders), and alcoholism may cease to be a problem. It should be mentioned that it is extremely difficult to recognize an underlying psychosis in someone who is inebriated. Psychiatric evaluation is much more meaningful and reliable when an individual has been sober for at least a few days after a drinking bout.

Alcoholism may occasionally also be symptomatic of minor, neurotic states, for instance, chronic anxiety states. In such cases, however, the course is often not very different from what has been described as gradual seduction.

TREATMENT OF ALCOHOLISM

The treatment of alcoholism can prove frustrating. It will be less so, however, if patient and therapist can set up a series of limited goals which can be reached in stepwise fashion. We would say that the first goal in treatment is to attain sobriety; the second to attain extended periods of sobriety; the third goal to attain permanent sobriety or complete abstinence; the fourth, and much more distant, goal to seek a fundamental personality change which obviates excessive drinking behavior as a coping device.

How are these goals to be achieved? To begin with, there has to be some recognitioin either on the part of the alcoholic or of someone close to him that drinking has become a problem. The individual does not first have to "hit rock bottom." Nor does he have to seek treatment entirely willingly and in full recognition of his problem with alcohol. Treatment can be initiated even when the alcoholic has been forced to come for help, by pressure from his family, from his job, or from the courts. In fact, some maintain that treatment can progress more satisfactorily if there are firm but non-punitive external controls to help the individual attain and maintain sobriety.

Treatment of an individual addicted to alcohol should begin with a thorough physical and mental evaluation. We have already mentioned that such an evaluation can only be meaningful when the person has not been drinking for at least several days. Since many alcoholics seek treatment while intoxicated, they may first have to be withdrawn from alcohol, or in the parlance of the alcoholic and those who treat alcoholics routinely, be "dried out." Often this can be accomplished only by hospitalizing the person for a short period of time.

In evaluating the alcoholic, one should pay attention to any physical damage (see Medical Complications, below) which has already been sustained; but the degree of reversibility of such damage needs also to be assessed. It is important for the doctor and the patient to know whether any significant organic damage has been done. The specific psychological and situational factors responsible for the excessive drinking must be identified in so far as possible. But an assessment of the sick parts of the personality is not enough. One must also discover by what strengths, through what resources or adaptive skills, the individual can once more be helped to face his life situation without resorting to drink. Only when all these factors are known, can an appropriate treatment plan be set up.

Educational, spiritual, and psychotherapeutic (individual and group, supportive and insight-oriented) treatment approaches have been developed. What specific form of treatment is to be chosen in any one case depends on its availability in a given location, as well as on the patient's receptivity to it.

Individual Psychotherapy

The individual psychotherapeutic approach is limited because of financial and manpower considerations. Many alcoholics, partly as a consequence of their disorder, cannot afford to pay for individual psychotherapy. On the other hand, even if the 15,000 fully trained psychiatrists in the United States spent forty hours a week, seeing forty alcoholic patients for one hour each, they would still only be able to see 600,000 or one-tenth of the total alcoholic population. Finally, individual psychotherapy demands a certain amount of tolerance for critical self-examination of which the alcoholic typically is not capable. For practical as well as theoretical reasons, therefore, on-going individual psychotherapy by a psychiatrist is only rarely the treatment of choice, with one major exception: where the cause of alcoholism is a specific, identifiable psychiatric disorder.

Alcoholism Treatment Centers

Community-based or community-centered alcoholism treatment centers represent the greatest advance by far in the treatment of alcoholism in the last two decades. They are now available in an increasing number of larger cities, and they are regionally available in rural areas. Such centers can provide initial medical and psychiatric evaluation, and, thereafter, on-going group therapy.

Group therapy can be helpful in the treatment of alcoholism in several ways. The group leader (usually a psychiatrist, a psychologist, or a social worker) can point up ways of handling emotional difficulties other than by drinking. Acceptance by him may be a source of considerable self-esteem for the alcoholic. More important than the group leader, however, are the group members, all people who, like himself, are trying to get along without drinking. He can understand them and feel understood by them in turn. Oftentimes a warm camaraderie grows up among group members which can provide the motivation for continued group attendance and continued sobriety from meeting to meeting. Persons whose basic problem is excessive dependency seem to benefit most from this approach; some dependency needs can be met in the group without harmful consequences.

The Spiritual Approach—Alcoholics Anonymous

Alcoholics Anonymous represents a non-medical, self-help approach. Developed in the mid-1930's in the United States, the method has spread throughout the world and there are some 12,000 groups with an estimated 350,000 to 400,000 members, of whom 20 per cent are outside the United States and Canada (11). The method is based on the notion that one alcoholic can affect another as no non-alcoholic can (3). It is essentially a spiritual approach. Alcoholics Anonymous tells the alcoholic who wishes to stop drinking that he has to accept the fact that he cannot help himself. He must, instead, rely on a "power greater than himself," how ever he wants to envision such a superior power. The group believes that the surest way to avoid drinking is actively to assist others to avoid drinking. There is no doubt that this approach has helped many alcoholics toward recovery and has saved lives, families, and much hardship. Not everyone, however, is able to accept and to benefit from the rather rigid system of A.A. When this is so, one of the other treatment approaches should be tried.

"Conversion" Experiences

A man has been drinking for fifteen years. He has wasted what money he had on alcohol. He has neglected his wife and children, physically as well as emotionally. One day he comes home drunk and finds his home in flames. As he stares at the scene he suddenly feels that he is to blame for their danger. Even as he rushes into the house he makes a promise that if his family can be rescued he will never touch drink again. With his help his wife and children do in fact escape from the flames and from that day forward he becomes completely abstinent.

Stories of such dramatic "conversion" experiences may seem incredible, yet they are not uncommon among recovered alcoholics. By their very nature they cannot be arranged or prescribed and are therefore largely outside of the repertoire of psychiatrists. The crucial experience need not necessarily have religious overtones, but it must have great impact.

MEDICAL COMPLICATIONS OF ALCOHOLISM

Excessive alcohol intake continued over a period of years can result in significant disease in a number of organ systems. Systems most frequently affected are the central and periphcral nervous systems, the gastro-intestinal tract, and the liver. The most important complication of alcoholism is cirrhosis of the liver, which in turn can predispose or lead to esophageal varices, hepatic coma, or cancer of the liver, all of which can cause death. Gastrointestinal complications include frequent episodes of acute alcoholic gastritis, increased frequency of peptic ulcer and of chronic pancreatitis. Malnutrition, particularly deficiency of the B vitamins, is frequently associated with prolonged excessive drinking. This in turn can cause damage to the central and peripheral nervous systems. These complications, with the exception of those affecting the central nervous system, will not be discussed here in detail. They are well covered in general medical texts and are mentioned here only for completeness. Those affecting the central nervous system, however, are of importance to the psychiatrist and will be elaborated.

Delirium Tremens (D.T.s)

Delirium tremens is a unique complication of alcoholism which occurs only after a number of years of excessive drinking. It never occurs as a result of simple alcohol intoxication, no matter how severe. It has its onset either late in a drinking bout or else upon cessation of drinking. As such, it is felt by most investigators to be a withdrawal syndrome (12), analogous to the withdrawal syndrome evoked when opiates are withdrawn from the opiate addict (see below). The special characteristics of the two withdrawal syndromes are, however, quite distinct. It is also thought that fluid and electrolyte disturbances, occurring as a result of prolonged drinking, inadequate food and fluid intake, and possible vomiting, contribute to the development of delirium tremens.

Full-blown delirium tremens is characterized by a severe psychotic delirium and by marked tremulousness, the two principal features which give the syndrome its name. The tremulousness affects the entire body musculature; the reflexes are hyperactive, and occasionally grand mal convulsions occur, which may, still more rarely, be fatal. The psychotic delirium is characterized by marked disorientation, confusion, severe anxiety, and by visual and auditory hallucinations, which are often frightening to the patient. In general, the patient appears acutely ill, his body temperature is raised moderately, and his heart beats rapidly. Early recognition and adequate treatment in a hospital can prevent or minimize the symptoms of delirium tremens.

Treatment is directed toward providing adequate sedation, restoring fluid balance and adequate vitamin and caloric intake. In the past, paraldehyde, a drug similar in composition to alcohol, was used for sedation in D.T.s. More recently, however, this has been replaced by one of the phenothiazine drugs, such as Sparine or Thorazine, for instance, or by large doses of chlordiazepoxide (Librium, 50 mgm intramuscularly initially, followed by oral doses of 25–50 mgm orally every six hours) (13, 14). With treatment the manifestations of delirium tremens gradually subside over a period of two to three days.

Korsakoff's Psychosis

After years of excessive drinking a certain portion of alcoholics develop irreversible brain damage. All the intellectual functions become impaired, but memory is particularly severely affected. As a result the individual elaborates an intriguing adaptive mechanism to cope with his memory deficit: confabulation. Fictitious memories are substituted for real memories which cannot be recalled (15). Although this syndrome has been called a psychosis (Korsakoff's psychosis, after the Russian neurologist who first described it), it is for the most part only a simple dementia, with severe memory loss, and only rarely is there psychotic elaboration. The reader is referred back to Chapter 4, Organic Brain Disease, for a discussion of dementia in general and its relation to superimposed psychosis. Most investigators feel that the syndrome is the result of long-standing vitamin deficiency associated with heavy drinking, but there is also some evidence to suggest that a direct toxic effect of alcohol on brain cells may play a role (16). The syndrome is not reversible, although it tends to stabilize if drinking is discontinued and good nutrition is restored. If the process has advanced to such a degree that the affected individual is no longer able to care for himself, hospitalization for prolonged care is indicated (17).

Alcoholic Hallucinosis

Alcoholic hallucinosis is another complication of alcoholism. It is characterized by episodes of auditory hallucinations in the presence of a clear sensorium. The voices, which are often described as accusatory and threatening, are in this sense very similar to those experienced by schizophrenic individuals. In fact, it has not been clearly established that alcoholic hallucinosis is something other than a manifestation of schizophrenia in an individual who has also become alcoholic. Both disorders occur with sufficient frequency to permit such an explanation, but the question has not been settled entirely. Therapeutically, the syndrome responds fairly well to hospitalization and treatment with one of the major tranquilizers, e.g. Thorazine. Recurrences, however, are frequent.

THE FATE OF ALCOHOLICS

It should be apparent from what has been said thus far that alcoholism is a serious disorder. In conclusion we want to consider the long-term outcome of alcoholism. Basing his conclusions on a retrospective study of 500 alcoholics, Lemere paints a rather grim picture (18). Since little formal treatment was available to the alcoholic at the time of this study (1953), the findings may be indicative of the outcome of alcoholism when untreated. Of his group, only 11 per cent became abstinent later in life. An additional 10 per cent were able to moderate their drinking somewhat as they grew older. The remainder drank to excess until their death, with about half of these becoming abstinent only during their final illness. Twenty-eight per cent died prematurely, either as a direct or indirect result of alcoholism: 17 per cent died of medical complications of alcoholism, 11 per cent committed suicide. This high rate of suicide among alcoholics has also been reported by other investigators (19). A more recent study (1966) from England compares the outcome of treated and untreated alcoholics, followed for a period of over six years (20). The rate of suicide was twice as high in the untreated as in the treated group, as was the rate of death from medical complications of alcoholism. It has been estimated that alcoholics die on the average ten years before their time, although any given alcoholic individual may live to attain a ripe old age.

NARCOTIC ADDICTION

A narcotic is a drug which in moderate doses relieves severe pain and anxiety and induces pleasurable lethargy and sleep. When used repeatedly, increasing doses are required to produce the same effects, a phenomenon known as tolerance. When used regularly and in increasing amounts, the user soon develops a physiological need for the drug (physiological dependence), which is manifested by the appearance of distressing abstinence or withdrawal symptoms upon discontinuation of the drug. When used in excessive amounts (overdoses), a narcotic can cause profound stupor or death. The narcotics under discussion include opium and opium derivatives, particularly morphine, and a group of synthetic drugs which have pharmacological properties essentially identical to those of the opiates. These drugs are used by physicians for the temporary relief from pain in acute medical emergencies, particularly the pain associated with an acute heart attack or certain accidental injuries or battle wounds. They may also be used against the continued pain experienced by certain patients dying of disseminated cancer. The regular (at least once a day) use of narcotic drugs outside of these situations represents drug addiction. It is characterized by craving for and psychological dependence upon the drug, as well as by tolerance and physiological dependence. In narcotic addiction the drug comes to be used to such an extent that the individual or society, or both, is harmed.

Narcotic addiction differs from addiction to alcohol in a number of respects, some of which are related, directly or indirectly, to the differing pharmacological properties of the drug. Narcotics produce much more intensely pleasurable effects than alcohol. Physiological dependence develops much more rapidly, and tolerance is much greater and develops more quickly with narcotics than with alcohol. Beyond this, the user of narcotics is from the outset in conflict with culturally established norms, whereas the user of alcoholic beverages can drink for extended periods of time without coming into conflict with society. Another fact is that while alcohol is readily and legally obtainable, narcotics, for other than specific medical indications, can be obtained only illegitimately and at great cost. The high price of illegally obtained narcotics leads addicts to commit innumerable crimes against property (theft, burglary, forgery) in order to be able to pay for a continued supply of drugs. Narcotic addiction is thus not only a psychiatric problem but a law enforcement problem as well.

The history of narcotic addiction in this country and throughout the world makes for interesting reading (21) but is beyond the scope of this chapter. We want to focus on narcotic addiction as it exists now in the United States and adduce only those historical highlights which are indispensable to a discussion of our present problem. Several events in particular stand out. The first of these is the invention of the hypodermic syringe around the middle of the nineteenth century. This led first to the use of the intramuscular route and later to the intravenous route of narcotic drug administration, which enhanced the pleasurable effects of the drug dramatically but at the same time produced much earlier and much more certain enslavement to the drug habit. The second event of importance to the course of narcotic addiction in this country was the passage in 1914 of the Harrison Narcotics Act, a federal law which provides for legal strictures against the sale and traffic of narcotic drugs. The law has been used to deal with narcotic addiction from a legal or criminal point of view. A third important event occurred when the federal government in the early 1930's authorized and had constructed hospital facilities for the treatment and rehabilitation of narcotic addicts and research facilities for the scientific study of the addiction problem.

TYPES OF NARCOTIC ADDICTION

As with addiction to alcohol, all individuals addicted to narcotics are not alike. Nevertheless several patterns of addiction can be distinguished which have differing implications for prevention, treatment, rehabilitation, and control (22).

The Street Addict

"Street addicts" make up the largest portion of narcotic addicts in the United States. They conform most closely to the stereotype of the narcotic addict. They are, for the most part, young men and women from underprivileged minority groups (Negroes, Puerto Ricans, first-generation Americans) who live in the poorer sections of some of our largest cities (New York, Chicago, Detroit, Washington, Los Angeles, San Francisco). These individuals become addicted early in life, either during adolescence or early adulthood, but in many cases before any work identity or work skills have been established. Typically they first started to use narcotics "for kicks," at the urging of their already addicted contemporaries. But not everyone who comes into contact with narcotics becomes addicted. There must be in the individual a special readiness for the drug. We have already described such readiness in the discussion of "instant addicts" in the section on alcoholism. Persons who have been unable to find a place in society and who have been unable to extract satisfying and meaningful experiences from ordinary living, succumb readily to the lure of drugs. They return to them over and over again, while all other activities and goals recede into the background. It should be pointed out, however, that positive pleasure is derived from the use of narcotics only in the early stages of addiction; once physiological dependence has become established the addict must use drugs primarily to avoid the intense discomfort of abstinence symptoms (see below).

The specific drug most commonly used by these addicts, both by choice and availability, is heroin, a derivative of morphine. Heroin may not be manufactured or sold in the United States legally. All the heroin in the United States is smuggled into this country and distributed illegally to addicted individuals at a high price. The cost of an average daily supply of heroin may run between fifteen and fifty dollars. Since few addicts have jobs or other legitimate sources of income, most resort to crime. They steal, rob, write false checks, play confidence games, or become small-time dealers in narcotics in order to assure themselves of a supply of drugs; many of the women become prostitutes. Although addicts often are quite skilled in the execution of their crimes, nevertheless they frequently are caught, brought to trial, and sentenced to jail. For some, the enforced abstinence from drugs experienced in prison can become a starting point toward a more normal life. For others, the prison experience may be embittering and provide further reason or excuse to return to drug use in the outside world.

Most such addicts associate primarily with other addicts, thus forming their own subctulture, with its own identity, code of conduct, even with its own language. One of the most meaningful terms in the addict's argot is "the street" (23). Because much of the addict's life centers on fleeting contacts with pushers and other addicts on street corners, this phrase has come to stand for all the pleasures, thrills, isolation, depravity, and misery of being addicted to narcotics.

The White Southern Addict

A second pattern of addiction has been identified among middle-class white persons. These individuals differ markedly from typical "street addicts." They are on the whole fairly well integrated into their communities and do not belong to an addict subculture. They live in towns scattered across the country, but the majority reside in the Southern states.* They become addicted somewhat later in life, often following the administration of narcotics by a doctor for the relief of pain. Finding that narcotics

---

* Why this pattern of addiction should be more common in the South is not at all clear.

fill a vital psychological need in their lives, they then continue to demand and obtain narcotics prescriptions from their doctors, who either do not recognize that their patients have become addicted or do recognize it and feel guilty for having introduced them to narcotics in the first place. Some of these patients will fake painful medical illness or use many doctors to obtain the necessary prescriptions, and occasionally will steal and forge prescriptions or even steal narcotics from drug stores or medical bags. On the whole, however, they are not so steeped in criminal activity as street addicts. Many are able to lead fairly productive lives, despite their addiction (24).

Professional Addicts

Persons who in their professional work have ready access to narcotic drugs are particularly vulnerable to narcotic addiction. Thus doctors, nurses, and pharmacists make up a disproportionately large fraction of all addicts. The greater emotional demands upon persons in the medical field have also been blamed for the higher incidence of narcotic addiction, but these alone would not be sufficient were it not for the easy access that health professionals have to narcotic drugs. Not that a breach of the law is not involved here, but it is of a different quality from that found in "street addicts." Professional persons who have become addicted will falsify narcotic records, steal from hospital supplies, write prescriptions using fictitious names, etc. When finally discovered, professional and legal sanctions are applied against them, and again the personal losses and the losses to society are great (25, 26).

These three patterns of addiction account for the majority of narcotic addicts, but not for all of them. Persons from all walks of life can become addicted. From a public health point of view it is important to know these over-all patterns of addiction. In dealing with individual patients the particular circumstances leading to addiction in that individual assume greatest importance.

Treatment of Narcotic Addiction

Treatment of narcotic addiction consists of two phases. The first is the detoxification or withdrawal phase; the second is the rehabilitation phase. Detoxification, the more dramatic of the two, can be accomplished quickly and with relative ease. Rehabilitation, a much more prolonged and more difficult process, taxes the ingenuity of the most skillful therapists.

Detoxification or Withdrawal

Withdrawal from narcotics can be carried out only in a drug-free environment. A "closed" hospital ward is best suited for this purpose to avoid the surreptitious introduction of drugs. For drug addicts, although they willingly submit themselves to treatment, only too readily change their minds once abstinence, or withdrawal, symptoms have made their appearance.

The Abstinence Syndrome

Within twelve to twenty-four hours after the last drug dose, abstinence symptoms make their appearance. Their severity depends on the amount and frequency of previous drug usage. The syndrome begins with an increase in anxiety and a general autonomic disturbance, characterized by the need to yawn and to stretch, by watery eyes, and a runny or stuffy nose. With the passage of time other, more distressing, symptoms make their appearance which, taken together, add up to a syndrome not unlike a severe case of flu: there is generalized muscular aching, crampy abdominal pain, nausea, vomiting, and diarrhea; chilly sensations, shivering, and goose flesh, along with generalized restlessness; the pupils become widely dilated and fail to respond to light; body temperature rises slightly and the pulse is fast. Unlike alcohol withdrawal, convulsions do not occur.

Substitution Therapy

When a patient has been using sizable quantities of a narcotic regularly, it is both humane and medically sound to withdraw him from it gradually. This is done by substituting methadone, itself an addicting drug, for the drug previously used by the addict. Given in doses of 15 to 20 mgm daily, the drug is gradually reduced over a period of three or four days, and the patient under these circumstances experiences only minimal discomfort. For many addicts, however, even this procedure is not necessary, since many have been taking only very weak, very dilute narcotic drugs, and as a consequence they have only mild withdrawal symptoms. During the period of withdrawal from narcotics, close attention must be paid to fluid and food intake. Most addicts are emaciated when they finally seek hospital treatment, and adequate nutrition must be re-established as quickly as possible.

Rehabilitation

Ideally, we would like to help the addict attain a life free of drug use which is at the same time personally satisfying and useful to his community. How this is to be accomplished, or whether it can be accomplished at all, is a matter of great controversy. In fact, few questions in psychiatry evoke such strong emotions or biases as this one. We can only conclude that no truly satisfactory answer exists as yet.

Lexington

We would like to describe one program for the treatment and rehabilitation of narcotic addicts in some detail. This is the program at the U. S. Public Health Service Hospital at Lexington, Kentucky. Because of its large size (1000 beds) and relatively long and distinguished history (the hospital opened in 1935) it is the program with which others must be compared. Narcotic addicts may be admitted to Lexington as voluntary patients, or they may be sent there as prisoner patients if they have been convicted of law violations in connection with their addiction. It should be made clear that being an addict is not a violation of the law, but that possession of illegally obtained drugs or selling of illegal narcotics is by law punishable.

In order to maintain a drug-free environment, the hospital is operated as a "closed" institution. Following admission, patients are withdrawn from narcotics, either gradually (substitution therapy) or all at once, depending on the degree of their addiction. Next they are given individual psychiatric and psychological evaluations in order to tailor the rehabilitation program to individual needs. To the degree that professional manpower is available, patients are offered individual or group psychotherapy. All patients physically able to work are given regular work assignments within the hospital. All patients have regular opportunities for recreational and creative expression. Basic educational and vocational skills are also taught.

It is of great interest that narcotic addicts living in this kind of environment, free of drugs, are by no means unhappy. In fact, this structured and protected setting allows many of them to function at levels higher than they had ever attained before. Unfortunately, this does not mean that they will not return to the use of drugs when they are once more outside the hospital and drugs are once more available to them. This point leads us to a consideration of prognosis in narcotic addiction.

OUTCOME OF NARCOTIC ADDICTION

Pessimism abounds in regard to the outcome of narcotic addiction. O'Donnell has pointed out, however, that the favorableness of results depends in large measure on the kind of criteria one uses to indicate favorable or unfavorable outcome (24). If one asks, how many addicts return to drug use at any time following any period of treatment or hospitalization, then the results are indeed discouraging: figures between 90 and 97 per cent have been quoted (27, 28). However, if one asks, how many addicts eventually abstain from drugs for significant periods of time (one year or more), then the results are a good deal more encouraging. Vaillant in his 12-year follow-up study on metropolitan street addicts found that approximately one-third were no longer using narcotics (29). O'Donnell's data on white southern addicts give an even more favorable impression. More than one-half were no longer using narcotics on follow-up (24). Both Vaillant and O'Donnell have presented data which indicate that the death rate in narcotic addiction is far higher than in the general population. It has been estimated that narcotic addiction, like alcoholism, reduces life expectancy by an average of ten years.

THE FUTURE OF NARCOTIC ADDICTION

The general public and professionals in the health field and in government agencies are keenly aware that current programs for the prevention and treatment of narcotic addiction are inadequate and that innovations and improvements are called for. The discussion of the nature of these changes, however, has been highly polemical, generating much heat and little light (30, 31). Extreme points of view are often presented. One of these is that narcotic addiction is purely a medical problem which should be dealt with at the discretion of the individual physician or of the medical profession as a whole. The other view is that narcotic addiction is a police problem, pure and simple: in order to deal with it more effectively, one need only use harsher and more effective police techniques. Unfortunately, it must be said that neither of these alone can be truly effective, and creative new integrations of these two approaches must be sought. A philosophical question is also involved: Should the rights of the individual addict or those of society come first? Again, we would say that, hopefully, approaches can be devised which will respect individual as well as societal rights.

While realizing the controversial nature of this matter, we would now like to join the discussion and add our own point of view. We would suggest that the several states and the federal government in the next few years enact laws to the following effect: Individuals addicted to narcotic drugs shall be compelled, under civil, not criminal, law to undergo detoxification and rehabilitation in hospitals especially designed for these purposes. The programs in these facilities shall be geared toward helping the addict become integrated or re-integrated into the workaday world of his community, by helping him to increase his vocational, educational, and interpersonal skills, and by helping him, through individual and group psychotherapy, to discover ways of dealing with external or internal problems other than by taking drugs. Such mandatory hospitalization shall be of at least six months' duration and shall be followed by mandatory supervision in the patient's community. Supervision shall have two purposes. First, to assure that the ex-addict does not return to drug use; and second, to assist him in finding suitable employment and housing and to continue to help him solve his problems realistically rather than with drugs. If while under community supervision an addict nevertheless returns to drug use, he shall again be compelled to enter hospital facilities for such additional time as will make drug-free existence in his community possible for him. California has already put into effect a program similar to what we have outlined here, and, in our opinion, to good effect.

ADDICTION TO BARBITURATES AND OTHER SEDATIVES

Barbiturates are sedative drugs which are commonly prescribed to induce sleep. They are also used in the treatment of convulsive disorders. They, too, have addiction potential in that psychological dependence, tolerance, and physiological dependence can occur. Barbiturate addiction may develop as an outgrowth of the treatment of chronic insomnia in anxious and dependent persons. Occasionally, narcotic addicts will substitute barbiturates when narcotics are unobtainable and thus become addicted to a second drug. Barbiturate addiction is in some respects a more serious disorder in that withdrawal from barbiturates can cause convulsions which are sometimes fatal (32). When physiological dependence on barbiturates has developed, gradual withdrawal is always indicated in order to minimize the risk of convulsions. Whereas persons taking narcotic drugs retain a clear sensorium, persons on chronic doses of barbiturates develop a chronic delirium, with intellectual and memory deficit, and have difficulty with equilibrium, which may cause them to fall and thus sustain bruises, broken bones, and head injuries.

Addiction has also been reported to a number of other hypnotic and sedative drugs. These include glutethimide (Doriden), meprobamate (Miltown, Equanil), ethchlorvynol (Placidyl), and a number of others. Glutethimide is particularly dangerous since the lethal dose is not much greater than the therapeutic dose (33, 34).

OTHER DANGEROUS DRUGS

Several other psychologically active drugs exist which do not produce physiological dependence but to which psychological dependence can readily develop. Regular use can lead to serious disorders of thinking, feeling, and behaving which can become dangerous to the user as well as to those around him. In particular, long-standing use of amphetamine, a stimulant drug, can cause psychotic states which are difficult to separate from schizophrenia (35). Chronic use of cocaine causes severe delirium and massive anxiety, as a result of which the user many harm himself or others. LSD can also produce psychotic states, some of which are not reversible (36). The dangers of this powerful drug far outweigh any potential beneficial effect. Marijuana is dangerous primarily because its use is often a first step toward more serious involvement with dangerous or addicting drugs.

MULTIPLE ADDICTIONS

In the last two decades increasingly large numbers of persons have been found to be using more than one addicting or dangerous drug, either simultaneously or in sequence. For this reason, when addiction to one drug is discovered, inquiry should also be made about the use of other drugs; for the treatment implications of all the addictions, though related, are not the same.

REFERENCES

1. World Health Organization, Expert Committee on Mental Health (Alcoholism Sub-committee). Second Report. W.H.O. Technical Report Series No. 48, 1952.
2. E. M. Jellinek, *The Disease Concept in Alcoholism,* Yale University Press, New Haven, 1960.
3. Alcoholics Anonymous. "The Story of How Many Thousands of Men and Women Have Recovered from Alcoholism," Alcoholics Anonymous Publishing, Inc., New York, 1955.
4. American Medical Association, Committee on Alcoholism of the Council on Mental Health. *Manual on Alcoholism,* A.M.A., Chicago, 1957.
5. Barry A. Kinsey, *The Female Alcoholic,* Charles C. Thomas, Springfield, Ill., 1966.
6. M. Keller and U. Efron, "The Rate of Alcoholism in the USA, 1954–1956," *Quart. J. Stud. Alcohol,* 19:316–19, 1958.
7. U. S. Bureau of the Census, *Statistical Abstracts of the United States: 1966* (87th Edition), Washington, D.C., 1966.
8. David J. Pittman, editor, *Alcoholism,* Charles C. Thomas, Springfield, Ill., 1959.
9. David J. Pittman and Charles R. Snyder, editors, *Society, Culture, and Drinking Patterns,* John Wiley, New York, 1962.
10. E. M. Jellinek, "Phases of Alcohol Addiction," *Quart. J. Stud. Alcohol,* 13:673–84, 1952.
11. Alcoholics Anonymous, General Service Office, personal communication, 1967.
12. Maurice Victor and R. D. Adams, "The Effect of Alcohol on the Nervous System," *Association for Research in Nervous and Mental Dis., Research Proceedings,* 32:526, 1953.

13. William T. Hart, "A Comparison of Promazine and Paraldehyde in 175 Cases of Alcohol Withdrawal," *Amer. J. Psychiat.*, 118:323–7, 1961.
14. Douglas W. Thomas and D. X. Freedman, "Treatment of the Alcohol Withdrawal Syndrome," *J.A.M.A.*, 188:316, 1964.
15. M. Victor and P. J. Yakovlev, "S. S. Korsakoff's Psychic Disorder in Conjunction with Peripheral Neuritis, A Translation of the Original Article," *Neurol.*, 5:394–406, 1955.
16. Maurice Victor, *et al.*, "A Restricted Form of Cerebellar Cortical Degeneration Occurring in Alcoholic Patients," *A.M.A. Arch. Neurol.*, 1:579–688, 1959.
17. Benjamin Malzberg, *The Alcoholic Psychoses. Demographic Aspects at Midcentury in New York State,* Yale Center of Alcohol Studies, New Haven, Conn., 1960.
18. F. Lemere, "What Happens to Alcoholics," *Amer. J. Psychiat.*, 109:674–6, 1953.
19. N. Kessel and G. Grossman, "Suicide in Alcoholics," *Brit. Med. J.*, 2:1671–2, 1961.
20. R. E. Kendell and M. C. Staton, "The Fate of Untreated Alcoholism," *Quart. J. Stud. Alcohol*, 27:30–41, 1966.
21. Lawrence Kolb, *Drug Addiction,* Charles C. Thomas, Springfield, Ill., 1962.
22. John A. O'Donnell and John C. Ball, editors, *Narcotic Addiction,* Harper & Row, New York, 1966.
23. Alexander A. Weech, Jr., "The Narcotic Addict and 'the Street'," *Arch. Gen. Psychiat.*, 14:299–306, 1966.
24. John A. O'Donnell, "A Follow-Up of Narcotic Addicts," *Amer. J. Orthopsychiat.*, 34:948–54, 1964.
25. Peter L. Putnam and Everett H. Ellinwood, Jr., "Narcotic Addiction among Physicians: A Ten-Year Follow-Up," *Amer. J. Psychiat.*, 122:745–8, 1966.
26. Herbert C. Modlin and Alberto Montes, "Narcotic Addiction in Physicians," *Amer. J. Psychiat.*, 121:358–65, 1964.
27. H. J. Duvall, B. Z. Locke and L. Brill, "Follow-Up Study of Narcotic Addicts Five Years after Hospitalization," *Public Health Rep.*, 78:185–93, 1963.
28. G. H. Hunt and M. E. Odoroff, "Follow-Up Study of Narcotic Drug Addicts after Hospitalization," *Public Health Rep.*, 77:41–54, 1962.
29. George E. Vaillant, "A Twelve-Year Follow-Up of New York Narcotic Addicts: I. The Relation of Treatment to Outcome," *Amer. J. Psychiat.*, 122:727–37, 1966.
30. Alfred R. Lindesmith, *The Addict and the Law,* Indiana University Press, Bloomington, Ind., 1965.
31. Dale C. Cameron, "Addiction—Current Issues," *Amer. J. Psychiat.*, 120:313–19, 1963.
32. Harris Isbell, *et al.*, "Chronic Barbiturate Intoxication. An Experimental Study," *Arch. Neurol. and Psychiat.*, 64:1, 1950.
33. William E. Bakewell and A. Wikler, "Non-Narcotic Addiction: Incidence in a University Hospital Psychiatric Ward," *J.A.M.A.*, 196:710–13, 1966.
34. John A. Ewing and William E. Bakewell, "Diagnosis and Management

of Depressant Drug Dependence," *Amer. J. Psychiat.*, 123:909–17, 1967.
35. P. H. Connell, *Amphetamine Psychosis*, Chapman & Hall, London, 1958.
36. Sidney Cohen, "A Classification of LSD Complications," *Psychosomatics*, 7:182–186, 1966.

8

Psychiatric Problems Associated with Old Age

INTRODUCTION

Aging is a continuous *process*. It begins even before birth and continues throughout the life span. *Old age,* on the other hand, is a limited period of life. It lasts anywhere from a number of years to a number of decades and *constitutes the final phase of the life cycle* (1).

Various chronological ages (60, 65, 70) have been said to mark the onset of old age, but chronological age is not an ideal criterion, since individual differences between persons of the same age can be great. For this reason, and for our purposes here, we would like to suggest instead *a constellation of experiences* which mark, in a more meaningful way, the beginnings of old age. We suggest that old age begins with a series of losses of capacities and activities, activities which have up to this point in time been of central significance in the life of the individual. Among these losses we think three are of particular importance: *cessation of reproductive capacity; cessation of child-rearing activity; cessation of work productivity.*

A number of objections may immediately be raised to the criteria we have chosen: that these events do not occur at the same age in all persons, nor at the same time in both sexes; that they do not apply to all individuals (e.g., childless couples); that one of the criteria applies primarily to women; that another applies primarily to men; that they do not lend themselves readily to statistical analysis, to mention only a few. Valid though some of the objections may be, we nevertheless feel that these events are of central relevance to the majority of people as they enter old age.

Although we have de-emphasized it, we cannot leave chronological age out of the picture altogether. At all ages the number of one's years has a practical as well as a psychological impact, and no less so in old age. For this reason it is important to note at what age the events we have cited usually occur in our society.

Cessation of reproductive capacity occurs for most women somewhere in their middle forties, unless menopause has been surgically induced at an earlier age. For men the end of reproductive capacity probably occurs somewhat later, although precise data are not available. Fatherhood has been reported in men in their seventies and eighties, and the record is held by a man who fathered a child when he was ninety-four (2).

Most parents are somewhere in their middle fifties when cessation of child-rearing activity occurs, although the range of variation here is quite wide. By this time their children are completing their education, marrying, moving away.

Cessation of work productivity generally occurs in the middle sixties. It is determined at the present time largely by social security legislation, which provides for retirement at age sixty-five.

We have stated that old age begins with a series of losses. In fact, we feel that *loss and decline are the dominant themes of old age,* at least in our society. But at other phases of life losses occur, too, and hitherto cherished rights and privileges must be relinquished (dependency, parental support, parental guidance). Such losses in childhood, adolescence, and young adulthood are far outweighed by the gains realized (increased independence, prestige, power, sexual gratification). The losses one sees in old age, by contrast, are more numerous and more visible, the gains fewer and less apparent.

OTHER SIGNIFICANT LOSSES

To make the point clearer, it will be useful to mention some of the other losses and declines which are experienced with some regularity by older people. In doing so we should keep in mind that they are occurring in a culture which emphasizes and rewards youth, activity, and accomplishment.

First, almost all aged people experience a *decline in physical vigor* and stamina (3). This decline will be seen as all the more threatening when a person's self-esteem or his livelihood has depended on physical activity. Apart from a general decline in physical strength, increasingly larger numbers of elderly people develop specific and often severe and chronically disabling illnesses (heart disease, hypertension, arthritis, etc.) which further limit activities and involvement (4). Second, there is a gradual *decline in mental agility* in all aged persons (5, 6). This general mental decline attributable to aging may be compounded by the occurrence of specific diseases affecting the brain, such as cerebral arteriosclerosis or senile brain disease. Third, concomitant with retirement, many aged individuals experience significant *declines in income*, amounting for many to a drop of as much as 50 per cent from previous income levels (7, 8). Fourth, the *loss of loved ones through death* (friends, associates, spouses, and siblings) becomes a frequent experience in old age, and leads to a growing *loneliness and isolation* (9). Lastly, the death of others brings forcefully to mind *one's own impending and inevitable death.*

But loss is only one side of the ledger. Old age is not experienced in the same way by all people; nor are the various concomitants of old age, for instance, retirement, experienced by all in the same way. In fact, some of the very same changes and events we have listed as *losses* might well be viewed by some as distinct achievements or *gains.*

Taking events somewhat in the same order as before, let us look at this other side of the picture. The loss of reproductive capacity may represent for many a newly won sexual freedom, without fear of pregnancy and unwanted late-life offspring. The fact that the children are grown, that they have been educated and are able to make a life of their own, is for many a source of personal satisfaction. It may also relieve them of financial responsibility for education and living expenses. Retirement need not be a dreaded experience pervaded by feelings of uselessness. When individuals have prepared for it, in terms of financial security and through lifelong participation in leisure activity, then the retirement years can indeed be "golden years." While the loss of physical abilities has no compensation as such, the expectations of society in this regard are lowered accordingly, and most older persons can still perform at levels in congruence with society's expectations. Much the same is true of the gradual decline in mental capacity. Here, too, the expectations of society are lowered as the age of a person advances. Declines in income can be offset for many by a concomitant decline in necessary expenditures after retirement.

It is hardest of all to compensate for the loss of loved ones. This is especially true of the loss of the spouse, which for many aged persons is the most grievous assault of all. But even here, new relationships can be established, either with other aged persons or by a re-establishment of a closer relationship with one or another of one's grown children. Lastly, even one's own impending death can be dealt with by a philosophical attitude and by a "mannerly" acceptance of death's inevitability.

We can see that, as elsewhere in human affairs, given events in old age may have different meanings for different individuals. Regardless of whether the events of old age in the long run come to be viewed positively or negatively, they have to be dealt with in some way. *An adaptation has to be made.* The balance between success and failure of adaptation at any age depends on the interplay of a series of factors which may be briefly cited: the age-specific task set up for the individual by his biological inheritance (e.g. puberty, menopause) and by his cultural inheritance (e.g. retirement); the individual's biologically given (e.g. intelligence, physical stamina) and experientially determined (e.g. self-confidence) capacities for adaptation, including his past record of successes or failures in adaptation; adventitious factors, such as accidents, wars, economic depressions (e.g. the Great Depression of the 1930's), scientific or technological advances, or changes in political or legal structure (e.g. Medicare).

Normative Problems Associated with Old Age

The transition from one phase of the life cycle to another is never automatic, simple, or quick. In fact, it is likely to be associated with a good deal of temporary distress, uncertainty, and upheaval. It is only after a new adaptation has been made, appropriate to the changed circumstances, that equilibrium can be re-established. For some persons, of course, this fortunate resolution never takes place and there develop instead either the minor maladjustments or the major psychiatric disturbances of old age. These will be discussed more fully below. The point to be made here is that a certain amount of anxiety, concern, or even depression in response to specific changes in life circumstances is not necessarily to be interpreted as indicative of mental illness. Yet what happens at such crisis points is crucial for determining the ultimate adjustment to old age made by a given individual. For instance, the loss of income, the loss of prestige, and the unaccustomed amount of unstructured time which must be faced in retirement, may make for some upsetting moments in the life of even the most well-adjusted individual. If, however, health remains intact, interpersonal relationships are not simultaneously disrupted, and leisure activities gradually assume greater importance, then internal calm and self-satisfaction may quickly return.

Massive disruptions, especially when unexpected, may of course lead to more serious and more prolonged difficulties and require outside intervention to re-establish a tolerable balance.

Aging Successfully

We may ask what constitutes a criterion of successful aging. At the moment two rather widely diverging theories of successful aging are vying with one another (10). The first of these is the *activity theory*. It holds that successful aging means the maintenance "as far and for as long as possible of the activities and attitudes of middle age." The second of these is the *disengagement theory,* most prominently championed by Cumming and Henry (11). It holds that successful aging consists of "the acceptance and the desire for a process of disengagement from active life." There is truth in both of these theories. Yet neither of them can account for all of the observable data. There is of course no reason to assume that there is only one way of aging gracefully. The specific form of adaptation to old age probably depends more on previous life style, past experience, personal preferences, and cultural opportunities than on conformity to any theoretical model of successful aging. Whichever theory one may wish to follow, one can nevertheless observe that people in old age *are less involved* in the social, recreational, work, and economic life of their community than they were at a younger age. What is particularly interesting is that those who are most active and involved at younger ages continue to remain relatively more active in old age. We might say that there is a *conservative principle* at work. Here, as elsewhere, the past is prologue.

The Conservative Principle in Aging

This conservative principle applies not only to levels of activity and involvement but to other areas as well. For instance, persons highly skilled in communication and interpersonal relationships may tolerate fairly well a lessening of these skills through brain damage or lack of mobility or other disabling affliction. But others, less richly endowed from the start, may be seriously incapacitated by comparable decrements. In a similar vein, proportionate declines in intellectual functioning or in level of income may have disproportionate effects on different individuals, depending on whether their original levels were high or low.

Orderly Careers

Closely related to the conservative principle in old age is another concept, that of the *orderly career*, as discussed by Wilensky (12) and elaborated by Maddox (13). Perhaps half the individuals in the working force experience regularly progressive work histories, without major reversals or false starts. For a large portion of those with orderly careers, their job is the center of a larger, job-connected social and interpersonal area of functioning. For those people retirement from their jobs is much less threatening, since social contacts may continue well beyond job contacts. On the other hand in those for whom the job is merely a way of making a living, not a way of life, the loss of the job will create something of a vacuum. A more general corollary of the orderly career concept is that those who have been able to adapt successfully to changing life circumstances up to old age are likely to continue to make satisfactory adjustments, while those unable to master the problems of younger years may continue to experience difficulties as they grow old. Schuster's study of a 106-year-old man provides a good illustration of how a resourceful personality and a richly experienced life can have staying power even into extreme old age (14).

Optimal adjustment to old age, in our opinion, consists of adaptations that bring continued over-all life-satisfactions to the individual; are not in gross conflict with the expectations of society; and are essentially continuous with the individual's previous existence and self-concept.

Minor Maladjustments in Old Age

Minor maladjustments in old age are fairly common, and it is not easy to separate them clearly from what we have called normative problems of old age (15). One useful criterion is whether some form of outside help is necessary. But even this distinction breaks down; for certain normative problems, too, can be resolved more easily with the help of others. Most frequent are *adjustment reactions in response to situational crises* typical of old age: retirement, major illness of self or spouse, moves from one's home to an apartment or nursing home, among others. Diffuse and at times severe anxiety is the primary symptom in most instances, often with attendant insomnia, irritabilty, or agitation; at times, previously established patterns of neurotic behavior may become more exaggerated. For instance, there may be an increase in obsessive rumination or an inordinate preoccupation with minor physical complaints, where such tendencies had previously been part of the individual's personality. Almost by definition, these maladjustment states are reversible, either through the passage of time, through a favorable change in the environment, or through the empathic intervention of someone close to the afflicted individual. That someone can be a relative, pastor, neighbor, or psychotherapist. Occasionally, the use of tranquilizing medication during the time of upheaval hastens the recovery process.

More persistent or recurrent maladjustments are also seen in a considerable number of elderly persons. Recurrent periods of depression, lasting from a few minutes to a few days, are common (16). The individual feels discouraged, blue, or worried, or he may become disgusted with his own uselessness. Often these episodes occur in response to specific changes in the individual's life situation, or when he has been confronted in some way by his own decline. Older persons tend to respond particularly to contacts with young children, being buoyed up by them initially, but becoming depressed later on as they reflect on their own failing vitality.

MAJOR PSYCHIATRIC DISORDERS IN OLD AGE

We have already mentioned that loss is the dominant theme of old age, and the psychiatric disorders seen most commonly in old age are closely related to loss. They comprise, on the one hand, the major affective disorders of old age, related to psychological loss, and on the other hand, the chronic brain syndromes of old age, related to loss of brain substance.

Affective Disorders in Old Age

Affective disorders in old age probably do not differ markedly from those seen in younger years as discussed in Chapter 2. However, a few additional points can be made in regard to recognition, treatment, and prognosis of affective disorders in old age. It is only in recent years that psychiatrists have come to recognize that not all psychiatric disorders in old age are a matter of brain deterioration. In fact, approximately one-half the persons beyond age sixty admitted to private psychiatric hospitals have affective disorders, primarily severe depressions. It is also only recently that we have come to recognize that these disorders are as responsive to treatment in old age as they are in younger years, or very nearly so. All the treatment techniques, viz. electroconvulsive therapy, drug therapy, and psychotherapy, used in the treatment of severe depressions generally can be used in old age, with only a few modifications (17).

Chronic Brain Disease in Old Age

We have already discussed organic brain disease in considerable detail in Chapter 4. There we gave brief descriptions of dementia caused by cerebral arteriosclerosis and by senile brain disease, the two most frequent causes of chronic brain disease in old age. However, a few additional remarks about dementia in old age are in order. First, we must distinguish between uncomplicated dementia and dementia with superimposed psychosis. The former is characterized by disorientation, forgetfulness, poor recent memory, difficulty in concentration, and perhaps some habit deterioration; the latter by delusions, hallucinations, assaultive or abusive behavior, or extreme regression. Psychotic symptomatology appears either when the progression of dementia is extremely rapid, when the recognition of intellectual deficit is particularly threatening to an individual's self-concept, when the accustomed interpersonal supports of family and friends are withdrawn, or when marked degrees of anxiety are aroused in some other way. Anxiety is dealt with less effectively by individuals with dementia than by persons with normal brain function.

Simple dementia in aged individuals is fairly well tolerated by society. However, psychotic behavior is not tolerated and generally results in fairly swift sequestration of the afflicted individual in a mental hospital. This is unfortunate in a way, for the transition to an unfamiliar and frightening hospital setting may cause further anxiety and lead to further disorganization of behavior. On the other hand, hospitalization rather forcefully indicates that something is indeed wrong and in need of attention. It can be the starting point of concerted planning for the patient by the patient himself, by his family, his doctor, and perhaps other community agencies.

PREVENTION AND TREATMENT OF PSYCHOSIS IN OLD AGE

We still know very little about prevention of mental disorders. To date we have no effective techniques for averting the onset of brain tissue loss. However, psychotic episodes, occurring as out-growths of dementia, can be prevented in many cases, or if not prevented, treated. Basic to prevention is the recognition that old people have the same emotional needs as others. They, too, need warmth, affection, approval, and interpersonal security. With advancing age they are less able to secure these for them-selves and they become more dependent on others. As they be-come increasingly less able to do for themselves, others may need to make plans for them. Changes in living arrangements or in other life circumstances may become necessary. Such changes should be carefully planned in order to minimize anxiety and to preserve self-esteem.

If a psychotic reaction does occur, and the person has to be hos-pitalized, treatment should be initiated promptly. One of the phenothiazine drugs, such as Thorazine, in doses of 25 mgm four times daily, is often sufficient to allay anxiety and to terminate psychotic thinking. A well-structured, friendly, and unambiguous atmosphere in the hospital helps to restore orientation and speeds recovery. When equilibrium has been re-established, plans should be made with the patient and with his family to have the patient return to his home setting as soon as possible. If some supervision and care are required at home and family members are genuinely willing and able to give such care, this is an optimal solution. However, where this can be done only grudgingly, admission to a home for the aged may actually be preferable, and even then continued contact with relatives and friends should be strongly encouraged. In no case should elderly persons be abandoned by those close to them.

AFFECTIVE DISORDERS VS. ORGANIC BRAIN DISEASE

At this point we need to return briefly to the affective disorders of old age and compare them with organic brain disease; for from the point of view of prognosis it is extremely important to differentiate between them. The survival of patients over sixty, admitted to mental hospitals because of affective disorder, is just as good as for all persons of that age. On the other hand, of those over sixty admitted because of organic brain disease (cerebral arteriosclerosis and senile brain disease), only slightly more than half will survive the next six months, and only about one-fourth will survive beyond two years from time of admission (17). In short, affective disorders can be reversed whereas organic brain disease in old age tends to be progressive.

PSYCHOTHERAPY OF AGED PERSONS

Freud held that significant modification of personality structure was not possible after age forty (18). Other psychotherapists, too, have recommended that depth psychotherapy not be undertaken with persons past middle age. Their views are based on the impression that personality becomes relatively fixed during mature adulthood and thereafter cannot be changed very readily, even with skillful therapy. While these views are probably valid, it should be pointed out that they have not been systematically tested.

On the whole, however, there is rather general consensus that some modification of the usual psychotherapeutic techniques is required to serve the specific needs of the aged (15, 19, 20). For one thing, the therapist usually needs to take a much more active role than with other patients. A real relationship has to be formed quickly with the patient so that he can derive strength and approval from it. The therapist may counsel his patient, examine alternative courses of action with him, provide information on available services, or even give advice. He may bring in other helping agencies, such as welfare workers, visiting nurses, or volunteer agencies. He frequently works with the patient's entire family, exploring the feelings of relatives about the patient, educating them about old age, at times making suggestions about alterations in living arrangements. He will convey to the patient his empathic understanding of the predicaments of old age. As long as the elderly person knows there is still someone who cares and understands, he retains hope and thereby can tolerate many losses and deprivations.

REFERENCES

1. Erik H. Erikson, *Identity and the Life Cycle,* Psychological Issues, Vol. 1, No. 1, International Universities Press, New York, 1959.
2. Alex Comfort, *The Process of Ageing,* Weidenfeld and Nicolson, London, 1965.
3. Alex Comfort, *The Biology of Senescence,* Routledge and Kegan Paul, London, 1956.
4. E. V. Cowdry, editor, *The Care of the Geriatric Patient,* second edition, C. V. Mosby, St. Louis, 1963.
5. James E. Birren, *The Psychology of Aging,* Prentice-Hall, Englewood Cliffs, N.J., 1964.
6. Jack Botwinick, *Cognitive Processes in Maturity and Old Age,* Springer, New York, 1967.
7. Juanita M. Kreps, editor, *Employment, Income, and Retirement Problems of the Aged,* Duke University Press, Durham, North Carolina, 1963.
8. Jim Hyatt, "Retirement Sneaks Up," *Wall Street Journal,* March 16, 1967.
9. O. K. Timm, "Modern Trends in Psychiatric Care of the Geriatric Patient," *J. Amer. Geriat. Soc.,* 13:1025–31, 1965.
10. Robert J. Havighurst, "Successful Aging," *Gerontologist,* 1:8–13, 1961.
11. Elaine Cumming and W. E. Henry, *Growing Old,* Basic Books, New York, 1961.
12. H. Wilensky, "Orderly Careers and Social Participation: The Impact of Work History on Social Integration in the Middle Mass," *Amer. Sociolog. Rev.,* 26:521–39, 1961.
13. George L. Maddox, "Retirement as a Social Event in the United States," in John C. McKinney and Frank T. de Vyver, editors, *Aging and Social Policy,* Appleton-Century-Crofts, New York, 1966.
14. Daniel B. Schuster, "A Psychological Study of a 106-Year-Old Man," *Amer. J. Psychiat.,* 109:112–19, 1952.
15. Alvin Goldfarb, "Minor Maladjustments in the Aged," in S. Arieti, editor, *American Handbook of Psychiatry,* Vol. I, Basic Books, New York, 1959.
16. Ewald W. Busse, *et al.,* "Studies of the Processes of Aging. X: The Strengths and Weaknesses of Psychic Functioning in the Aged," *Amer. J. Psychiat.,* 111:896–901, 1955.
17. Martin Roth, "The Natural History of Mental Disorder in Old Age," *J. Ment. Sci.,* 101:281–301, 1955.
18. Sigmund Freud, "On Psychotherapy," in *Collected Papers,* Vol. I, Basic Books, New York, 1959.

19. Group for the Advancement of Psychiatry, Report No. 59. *Psychiatry and the Aged: An Introductory Approach*, New York, 1965.
20. Mathew Ross, "A Review of Some Recent Treatment Methods for Elderly Psychiatric Patients," A.M.A. *Archives of Gen. Psychiat.*, 1:578–92, 1959.

9

Psychological Reactions to Illness and Dying

Serious physical illness represents a major unfavorable change in life circumstances and as such demands a new psychological integration on the part of the afflicted individual. Not infrequently the impact of illness is so great that a smooth adaptation to it cannot be made, and instead there appear maladaptive responses, or psychiatric symptoms. These can further incapacitate the patient, interfere with his treatment, or slow his recovery. Serious illness, of course, usually affects not only the patient but his near relatives as well, some of whom may develop fleeting or lasting psychiatric symptoms.

What constitutes "serious" illness? Even minor illnesses may threaten the adjustment of individuals who tolerate poorly frustrations of any kind or who regard themselves as invulnerable and immune to illness. In general, however, we think of illness as being serious when it causes the patient great suffering and pain (for instance, trigeminal neuralgia); or when it is life-threatening (for instance, a heart attack or a perforated peptic ulcer); or when it is expected to be fatal (leukemia, cancer); or when it is likely to cause chronic disability (for instance, chronic deforming rheumatoid arthritis).

One other medical situation likely to have a major psychological impact on the patient is an illness, an accident, or a surgical procedure that *changes the person's external appearance* in some way, be it *for the better or for the worse*. Examples are such disfigurements as burn scars, trauma to the face or the hands, severe skin eruptions, and amputation of a limb or a breast because of malignant disease, and also such corrective or cosmetic procedures as plastic surgery to the nose, removal of an unsightly birthmark or scar, or surgical correction of a deviated eye or of a club foot. These procedures have particular impact because they require the person to change his image of himself, and hence alter his identity. Adverse psychological reactions in this situation are fairly common and can be of great variety and severity.

ADAPTIVE MECHANISMS IN RESPONSE TO ILLNESS

Illness constitutes a type of stress, and as such calls out adaptive or defensive operations in the afflicted individual. Whether the adaptation will be made successfully or not depends on the severity of the illness, the patient's general ability to handle stress, and the specific meaning the illness has for a given patient.

The Sick Role

Being sick is a ubiquitous experience, and since it always requires some kind of an adaptation or adjustment, most societies have developed a rather formalized, standard, and ready-made pattern of behavior which a person is expected to adopt when he falls ill. This ready-made pattern is the "sick role." The sick role has as its counter-role the "care-taking" role, which is adopted by other members of the society vis-à-vis the sick person. The nature of the sick role and that of the care-taking role differ widely from one culture to the next but they are always complementary to each other in a given culture.

In our society, when a person falls ill he acquires the right to be taken care of by other members of the society, either by relatives and friends if the condition is not too serious, or by professional care-taking persons, such as nurses and doctors, if the situation warrants. At the same time, the sick person is given leave—in some instances even required—to drop some of his usual responsibilities, such as the performance of his job or of his ordinary social and civic duties. In return, he is assigned a new set of responsibilities. These include seeking out medical care, "co-operating with the doctors," "going along with the treatment," and above all, implicitly and explicitly desiring and striving to get well.

In a serious illness, the adoption of the culturally prescribed sick role may suffice as an adaptive mechanism in the majority of instances. In others, additional mechanisms may be brought into play. Inability to accept the sick role, however, almost always indicates difficulty in dealing with the changed situation, and virtually guarantees the utilization of one or another of the more maladaptive responses to illness which we will discuss below.

Regression

Regressive behavior is that which is more appropriate to a small child than to an independent, responsible adult. A certain amount of regression is encouraged by the culturally prescribed sick role, and it no doubt aids in the healing and recovery process of most illnesses. At times, however, patients may overshoot the mark of desirable regression. They may develop a mode of behavior which is no longer socially tolerated and which may sabotage treatment and convalescent programs. Thus, some patients may become demanding, impatient, have temper tantrums, whine, talk baby-talk, refuse to co-operate, and in every way do the opposite of what is asked of them. In other words, they may behave not so much like sick children as like badly behaved and ill-mannered children. If physicians or members of the family fail to understand the significance of this behavior they may respond to the sick and regressed individual with anger and rejection, which will of course further distress the individual and lead to aggravation of his problem. As with naughty children, a firm yet tender, but non-punitive attitude is helpful, as are clearly stated expectations and anticipations. If it can be conveyed to the patient that others understand his distress and his fears of being ill, and that all that can reasonably be done for his illness is being done, then he may be able to accept his situation with greater equanimity.

Denial

Really serious illness, especially fatal and potentially fatal illness, and illness affecting major portions of the brain, often is dealt with through denial (1). The fact that illness, even grave illness, exists, is openly negated and all evidence to the contrary is swept aside. The gain from the use of this mechanism lies in the fact that the person does not at the moment have to face the consequences of his illness and does not become discouraged or depressed. Unfortunately, this denial may also lead to a refusal of treatment or to a refusal to co-operate with already instituted treatment which might in fact alleviate or even cure the condition. But denial, especially when used selectively and intermittently, can also play a positive role in coping with the impact of severe illness.

Depression

Depression is clearly the most frequent adverse response to serious illness. In various statistical studies the incidence of depression has been found to range from a low of 20 per cent to a high of 64 per cent (2, 3, 4). This variation may be accounted for by the fact that the authors of the different studies did not all employ the same criteria for a finding of depression, and the severity of illness in the patients studied was not constant from one study to the next. As we pointed out in the chapter on affective disorders, it is often difficult to decide at what point of severity depression is a mere fleeting everyday emotion, at what point it becomes a psychiatric symptom or syndrome (reactive depression), and at what point it becomes a full-blown psychiatric disease or disorder affecting the entire organism (definitive depression). The facts are that subjective sadness, low self-esteem, wanting to die, lack of interest in one's surroundings, a dim view of the future, and fits of crying, are frequently observed. Complete hopelessness, actual suicide attempts, suicidal ruminations, self-accusations, and depressive delusions (delusions of guilt, of poverty, of condemnation) occur more rarely; that is to say, few patients become depressed to the point of an affective psychosis. Those who do develop a definitive depression often give a history of previous severe depressive illness, or a family history of affective disorder or suicide.

Some authors liken the depressive reactions in medically ill patients to grief reactions, thereby implying that they are "normal" responses to the loss of one's good health. Though they may be normative in the statistical sense, they are nevertheless troublesome and merit medical attention. In fact, Engel, in a brilliant essay, has raised the question whether normal grief, so common in human experience, may not properly be considered a disease (5).

The depressive reactions concomitant with serious medical illness frequently respond to psychological intervention on the part of the patient's personal physician or of a consulting psychiatrist. All that is needed in many instances is to convey to the patient an empathic understanding of how being sick is affecting him, to listen to and to understand his concerns and fears. Additional clarification of the prognostic implications of the patient's illness may also be needed. Occasionally long-term psychotherapy is indicated. When a full-blown psychotic depression has developed, psychological intervention alone will probably not be effective, and drug-therapy or electroconvulsive treatment may be required. This should be considered when the patient is suicidal or when his depression interferes significantly with his ability to co-operate with his medical treatment.

DEATH AND DYING

Ehrenberg, the German biologist, has pointed out that death of the human organism is a biological necessity. In fact, all organisms which show any degree of differentiation are bound to die, while only certain one-cell organisms retain a kind of potential immortality (6). As a general scientific principle we can readily accept this. However, when applied to us personally, the necessity of our own death becomes much harder to bear. Except in adolescence and in extreme old age we rarely contemplate our own inevitable dying, and psychoanalytic studies indicate that in the unconscious we think of ourselves as immortal (7). Integrating the necessity of dying into one's life experience is the central task of many, if not all, philosophical and religious systems.

Our lives are defined by the moment of birth and the moment of death. Ordinarily we measure our life only in relation to its starting point, that is, we measure our years from the date of our birth. In some ways, however, the life remaining, i.e. the distance to death, is at least equally important, since it defines what can still be experienced or accomplished in our life. But we rarely allow ourselves to think in this way. In fact there is a general reluctance to face up to our ultimate dying. Jeffers and Heyman have made some very interesting observations in this regard (8). Working with persons sixty years old and over, they found that even people who stood near the end of their lives were very reluctant to admit that this was so. As part of a larger study on attitudes toward death, a group of subjects were shown a straight line and asked to indicate on it where they put themselves in relation to the beginning and the end of their lives. The majority, all over sixty and many in their eighties, marked the line somewhere near the halfway mark or, more rarely, two-thirds of the way toward death. Some admitted knowing that their lives were nearly over, but said that they wanted to "play it safe" and not to stack the cards against themselves by placing the mark too near the end of the line. This general reluctance to acknowledge death is also documented in Mitford's book on funeral customs in the United States (9).

Communication with Dying Patients

The fact that a person is dying or is rapidly approaching death sets him apart (10). On the one hand, people may be drawn to him by the common bond of their own mortality; on the other hand they may shy away from him because his dying reminds them of their own inevitable death. Even those who feel close to the dying person are often unable to bring themselves to discuss with him that which is uppermost in their minds—his dying. The result is that all too often he is left alone with his thoughts, his fears, and his feelings, without a way of settling or resolving them.

At no other point in life does a person need a continued relationship with another person more than when he is faced with the extinction of all his relationships. Yet it often happens that when it becomes clear that someone is fatally, that is, incurably ill, other people draw away. This is not done deliberately or maliciously by any means, although the effect may be no better than if it were. But to talk with a dying patient about dying is far too threatening for many people. To talk with him about matters of lesser significance may seem frivolous or otherwise inappropriate. The result is isolation, a breaking off of communication.

The doctor who is caring for the dying patient plays an important part in seeing to it that this does not happen. Much more is involved than the old question of whether or not the patient should be told "the truth" about his condition. What is far more important is the kind of communication which takes place between doctor and patient both before and after the doctor decides to tell or not to tell the patient "the truth." Fatally ill patients

often know that they are dying without having to be told (11).
Whether they know it on the basis of internal perceptions or on
the basis of noting the reactions of other persons toward them is
hard to decide in the individual case; both kinds of perceptions
probably contribute. So the question in many cases comes down
to whether or not to discuss with the patient openly what doctor
and patient each knows, separately and in isolation. This decision can only be made when the doctor understands a good deal
of the patient's psychological functioning. Doctors who *always* or
never tell fatally ill patients the truth are basing their decision
more on their own personality characteristics than on those of
their patients.

Quite understandably, doctors, who are dedicated to saving
lives, may themselves at times have difficulty facing a fatal outcome in one of their patients. But we would maintain that even
when a situation is medically hopeless, it need not be psychologically hopeless. Therefore the doctor should not withdraw from
the patient when all his technical skills have been exhausted.
Instead, he should continue to bring his human skills into play
(12).

In general, patients who can look back on a full and rich life,
a life which on balance has been successful and worthwhile, can
also accept death. Others, who have had difficulty in adapting
earlier in life, will "not go gentle into that good night," in the
words of the poet Dylan Thomas (13), but will go, kicking and
screaming, refusing to accept the personal application of a universal law. It is just these people who require the psychological
help of a skilled physician or psychiatrist in their final days.

REFERENCES

1. Edwin Weinstein and Robert Kahn, *The Denial of Illness*, Charles C.
   Thomas, Springfield, Ill., 1955.
2. J. M. Hinton, "The Physical and Mental Distress of the Dying Patient,"
   Quart. J. Med., 32:1, 1963.
3. Mark A. Stewart, Fenton Drake and George Winokur, "Depression
   Among Medically Ill Patients," *Dis. Nerv. System*, 26:479–84, 1965.

4. R. H. Dovenmuehle and A. Verwoerdt, "Physical Illness and Depressive Symptomatology. I. Factors of Length and Severity of Illness and Frequency of Hospitalization." *J. Geront.*, 18:260, 1963.

5. George L. Engel, "Is Grief a Disease?" *Psychosom. Med.*, 23:18–22, 1961.

6. Rudolf Ehrenberg, *Theoretische Biologie*, Springer, Berlin, 1923.

7. Sigmund Freud, "Thoughts for the Times on War and Death," in *Collected Papers*, Vol. IV, Hogarth Press, London, 1924.

8. Frances C. Jeffers and Dorothy Heyman, personal communication.

9. Jessica Mitford, *The American Way of Death*, Simon and Schuster, New York, 1963.

10. K. R. Eissler, *The Psychiatrist and the Dying Patient*, International Universities Press, New York, 1955.

11. Adriaan Verwoerdt, *Communication with the Fatally Ill*, Charles C. Thomas, Springfield, Ill., 1966.

12. Group for the Advancement of Psychiatry, Symposium No. 11. *Death and Dying: Attitudes of Patient and Doctor*, New York, 1965.

13. Dylan Thomas, *Collected Poems*, New Directions, New York, 1957.

10

Psychotherapy

INTRODUCTION

The subject of psychotherapy has already been mentioned a number of times in previous chapters. But we now come to a more systematic consideration of psychotherapy, since it is after all one of the major—or, in the view of some, *the* major—treatment modalities of psychiatry today. We want to look at its practical and theoretical aspects.

Actually, we should perhaps be speaking not of psychotherapy but of psychotherapies, in the plural, since there are a number of forms and varieties which differ in their practical application as well as in their theoretical underpinnings. We will confine our initial remarks now to more general considerations; later on we will take up several of these varieties.

DEFINITIONS

A modern dictionary (1) defines psychotherapy as "the science or method of curing psychological abnormalities and disorders by psychological techniques." On the basis of our own practical experience, as well as on theoretical grounds, we would alter that definition somewhat. We would say that psychotherapy is a method of beneficially influencing the course and outcome of disordered behavior by psychological techniques. As practising psychotherapists we cannot be so optimistic as to employ the word "cure." Rather, we must speak of amelioration, of renovation, or, as Colby does, of repair work (2). Colby goes on to state that the goal of psychotherapy is "to relieve the patient of distressing neurotic symptoms or discordant personality characteristics which interfere with his satisfactory adaptation to a world of people and events."

COMMON CHARACTERISTICS OF PSYCHIATRIC PATIENTS

If our aim as psychotherapists is to bring about beneficial changes in our patients we must first identify what in them needs changing. While the specific symptoms and underlying conflicts differ widely from patient to patient, we can nevertheless make several simple yet telling assumptions about persons who present themselves for psychotherapy.

First, we can safely assume that they all suffer from low self-esteem in some important area of their being. The fact that they have come to require psychiatric help can only have exaggerated this low opinion of themselves.

Second, we can assume that they at times make use of patterns of behavior which are more or less automatic, inflexible, stereo-typed, and which are not necessarily geared to the specific problem situation with which they are faced; their patterns are therefore impractical or maladaptive.

Third, we may assume that they are, in at least some significant area of their lives, out of touch with or unaware of their own feelings, impulses, and thoughts. These hidden feelings and thoughts may nevertheless influence their behavior in ways that the patients are unable to recognize, and hence unable to control.

Fourth, we can assume that psychiatric patients have experienced difficulty in their relationships with other people.

Although these characteristics appear disparate enough, they are closely related. The presence of one implies the presence of all. The various statements represent different levels of looking at interpersonal and intrapersonal functioning. Which level or approach the therapist will use with any given patient depends on many factors, some residing within the patient, some within the therapist.

THE PROCESS OF PSYCHOTHERAPY

Psychotherapy is practised between a person with some recognized emotional difficulty and a recognized psychotherapist. It is a *collaborative* effort in which patient and therapist alike are dedicated to the same task, namely, to the amelioration of the patient's difficulty in adaptation. It is not practised *upon* a patient, the way radiation therapy or surgery might be practised on a totally passive, though co-operative, patient. In this treatment the patient must participate *actively*. In fact, at times it may appear to the patient that he is doing all the work. When that is the case, it is likely that he is making solid progress.

Communication is the main vehicle by which psychotherapy is carried forward. An ongoing interchange between patient and therapist takes place, an interchange that is both verbal and nonverbal. From a purely descriptive point of view, the patient meets with the therapist over a period of time, usually on a regular basis, to discuss with the therapist what is troubling him about the conduct and course of his life. The therapist listens and responds in turn. The response may be in the nature of a clarifying question or of a comment designed to indicate that he has understood the patient's difficulty. As the therapist listens to the patient, he is interested not only in what the patient says but also in how he says it. As we have mentioned, psychiatric patients already suffer from low self-esteem which is likely to be made worse by having to see a psychiatrist. They will therefore be inclined not to reveal aspects of themselves of which they feel ashamed or for which they have been criticized or ridiculed in the past. This process of concealment may go on both consciously (intentionally) as well as unconsciously (unintentionally). It will be most prominent initially and will recur at certain highly significant stages of psychotherapy. Such concealment, however, is never complete. The patient's manner, his facial expressions, gestures, and changes in posture reveal to the alert therapist what the patient is trying to hide from the therapist and from himself. Ultimately, and with the help of the therapist, the patient may come to reveal himself to himself.

It is interesting that these non-verbal channels of communication remain open and effective even when communication along verbal lines has become blocked or distorted. In the same way that the therapist does not confine himself to heeding only the spoken words of the patient, he does not rely solely on the use of spoken words when he has something to communicate to the patient. His gestures, facial expressions, or changes in posture say much to the patient that cannot be put into words. For instance, when a psychiatrist pushes a box of Kleenex near the hand of a male patient who has been unable to cry over the death of his wife, more has been accomplished by thus giving encouragement and permission to cry than by any number of well-chosen words.

We have given a brief account of how psychotherapy is carried out. We may now ask what there is in this procedure which can lead to beneficial change. What are the "active ingredients" (3) of the psychotherapeutic process?

THE ACTIVE INGREDIENTS OF PSYCHOTHERAPY

Psychotherapy is such a complex process that it is not easy to separate one particular aspect of this process from the others, since they all occur more or less simultaneously. In addition, while someone is in psychotherapy, the rest of his life does not stop. Events outside of therapy go on and can influence adjustment significantly, favorably or adversely.

The question about "active ingredients" is a fairly recent one. Earlier it was assumed that a specific technique of psychotherapy, such as the gaining of insight, or the emotional re-living of an experience (catharsis), was specifically responsible for whatever improvement resulted. As the various forms of psychotherapy multiplied and became differentiated from one another, it became apparent that they were all effective to a certain degree. In fact, on closer study it became apparent that all the different therapies produced improvement in roughly the same percentage of cases, that is, in about 60 to 70 per cent. Still more startling was the observation that even among persons who sought psychiatric help but who received no specific psychotherapy or other psychiatric treatment, roughly the same proportion improved (4, 5).*

What could account for this? Were there perhaps common elements in all the different forms of psychotherapy—in psychoanalysis, psychoanalytically oriented psychotherapy, supportive therapy, advice-giving, drug-giving, even when no specific therapy was given at all? Several common factors can be delineated.

The Placebo Effect

First, it can be said that in each case the patient *expects* to be helped by coming to see the doctor. Could it be, then, that the mere expectation of improvement can actually result in improvement? The answer to this question is an unqualified "Yes." Technically this is called the placebo effect. A placebo is an inert medication or an inert technique, applied in a situation where active medication or clearly proven techniques are ordinarily applied. Shapiro (6) has made the point that until about a hundred years ago most medical practice was placebo practice. Few prescriptions (with the exception of morphine and a few others) had any specific pharmacological value, and many procedures, such as purging and bloodletting, were not only ineffective but sometimes dangerous. Yet doctors seemed to enjoy a high reputa-

---

* One of the difficulties of these data is that there is no generally agreed-upon method of assessing improvement from psychiatric difficulty, a problem to which we shall return when we are discussing the several different types of psychotherapy.

tion and patients seemed to get better under their care. It is likely that the physicians of those days were more able to benefit persons with psychological ills than with physical ones. The expectation of getting well must have played a large role then, as it does today. For some patients this expectation will be the determining factor in their improvement; for others its significance will be minor.

The Therapeutic Relationship

Another factor common to all the varieties of psychotherapy is the relationship that develops between patient and therapist in the course of treatment. This relationship is emphasized to a greater or lesser degree in the different therapies, but it is never absent. One variety of psychotherapy is in fact called relationship therapy. In other forms, such as in psychoanalysis, relatively little is made of the actual relationship between patient and therapist. Instead, it is viewed primarily as a projection screen for the patient's usual way of relating to people.

We have already said that the relationships of a neurotic individual with other people are apt to be poor. The relationship between patient and therapist becomes a proving-ground for the patient's skill in interpersonal dealings. His chances of success are greatly improved in this situation compared with situations he has previously encountered. The therapist, to the degree that he is able to attain this ideal, has no personal expectations of the patient; he has no axe to grind; he is accepting and non-critical of the patient. That, of course, does not mean that he accepts all that the patient does. Rather, he is trying to change certain maladaptive aspects of the patient's behavior. In psychotherapy, patients may thus discover that relationships between people need not be frightening, mutually destructive, overwhelming, or always competitive. For certain patients the therapy may represent an opportunity to establish a trusting relationship for the first time, or a relationship in which they are allowed to express their most private feelings without fear. Alexander (7) referred to this aspect of therapy as "emotional re-education."

In the safety zone of the therapeutic relationship, the patient may be able to allow himself to experience feelings and desires which he previously had to push out of consciousness. He can now begin to deal with them openly, rather than be controlled by them.

We agree with this emphasis on relearning to relate. The patient's experience in psychotherapy, may have significant carry-over to other relationships in his life. A satisfactory relationship with the therapist can of itself improve self-esteem. However, the real pay-off comes when the patient is able to take his newly won skill and confidence into relationships outside of therapy, especially into relationships which previously caused him great discomfort.

Breaking the Cycle

There is still another feature of psychotherapy which deserves to be called an active ingredient. It is the process which we will describe, perhaps somewhat clumsily, as "breaking the cycle." The cycle we are speaking of is the vicious cycle of neurotic behavior which has already been discussed in Chapter 5 of this book. It is self-perpetuating unless it is somehow interrupted. We now want to talk about the "somehow" of interrupting it. Any therapy worth its salt must do this in some way. Because it is a rather difficult concept, we will look at it in several ways.

In order to initiate change in a patient's behavior, *the therapist must respond to the patient in ways which are foreign to the patient's expectations.* We are not speaking of responses which are of themselves strange or shocking. Kindness to a man who expects rejection, acceptance to a man who expects criticism, or a polite distance to a woman who expects to be admired by every man, can have quite an impact. Let us illustrate: An angry young man is constantly unleashing verbal assaults on other people, including people with whom he would like to form close relationships. His attacks, of course, stand in the way of his desires and generally provoke a counter-attack from those whom he is attacking. We have no reason to assume that he will behave very differently in his first few contacts with a psychiatrist. If the psychiatrist responds to him in the anticipated manner, that is, with anger, then the patient's behavior will be reinforced. It will merely add fresh fuel to his anger, while his desire for a close relationship goes unfulfilled.

But if the psychiatrist responds in a novel way (novel in the patient's experience, that is), he will set the patient somewhat on his ear and force him to look at his behavior in a new light. We might say the psychiatrist is joggling the patient's defenses. Now the next move is up to the patient, who must find a new way of responding to this psychiatrist who refuses to act in the expected manner.

And here we come upon one of the most amazing phenomena of mental life. One might think that a patient would only be too glad to give up unrewarding and maladaptive patterns of behavior. But the facts are quite otherwise. Not only does the patient not want to change, but he wants other people to go on reacting to him as they have been. This resistance to change, this behavioral inertia, is one of the most fundamental properties of neurotic behavior. No matter how maladaptive a neurotic pattern may be, it nevertheless represents an established solution to a vexing problem. To give up this established solution would expose the patient to anxiety and renewed conflict, which he of course wants to avoid. He therefore clings to his old solutions with a tenacity which is truly amazing. It is as though he were hoping that by repeating the same (unsuccessful) performance over and over, he could finally force a more favorable outcome. Freud called this the *repetition compulsion*, a phenomenon which is one of the most serious obstacles to success in psychotherapy (8). Only gradually, as the patient begins to form a warm attachment to the therapist, and as he feels safe in this new relationship, can he recognize and gradually give up some of his old "security operations" and experiment with new ways of behaving.

We can also look at the process of "breaking the cycle" in another way. From the viewpoint of role theory we can say that in order to initiate change *the therapist must not play counter-role* to the patient's usual role. Let us again take an example: A middle-aged woman relates to other people primarily by being "nice" to them, unaware that she harbors deep resentments for most people, particularly for those who are better off than she is. Being unaware of her own hostilities she is amazed that people are not always as grateful to her for her kindnesses as she thinks they might be. She feels hurt that despite her many good deeds she actually has few friends. Bitterly, she redoubles her efforts at being kind to others. In this she goes to extremes, she "kills them with kindness," as the saying goes.

If she comes for psychotherapy she will be kind to the psychiatrist also, she will try to be "no bother" to him. She will compliment him on his professional reputation, or on his tie, or on his office furniture. The psychiatrist will not play counter-role to her role of "Being a Nice Lady." He will respond to her not with return compliments but with a serious investigation of the causes of her difficulties.

Regardless of how we want to look at the process of "breaking the neurotic cycle," we must realize that a single intervention or confrontation is not enough. This is a learning process and learning requires repetition; repetition and time. Is the passage of time, then, yet another active ingredient in successful therapy? Perhaps; but that is so self-evident that we will not dignify it with still another subheading.

What we have done in these last few paragraphs is to separate, somewhat artificially, the several aspects of psychotherapy which we think are crucial in bringing about change. In actual therapy they are not separated but are integrated parts of an organic process. We are certain, too, that we have not been able to identify all the "active" ingredients, and the ideas set down here on this point represent not a dogma but only a point of view.

Types of Psychotherapy

Supportive vs. Insight-Oriented Psychotherapy

In discussing various forms of psychotherapy a dichotomy is often drawn between supportive and insight-oriented psychotherapy. We feel that this is a valid distinction. But that does not mean that the one is practised exclusive of the other. It is a matter of the extent to which one or the other is emphasized. Tarachow (9) has drawn the distinction between the two more clearly than anyone else. The important difference is this: In insight-oriented psychotherapy the therapist does not satisfy any of the patient's needs directly. In response to the patient's demands for various satisfactions (for friendship, for admiration, for advice, for control, etc.), the therapist does not respond by acceding to the demands but wonders with the patient why he is making these specific demands in this specific way. He analyses, or interprets, but he does not "give" to the patient. Insight therapy is need-frustrating then, in a sense, rather than need-satisfying. This means that a great deal is asked of the patient who has to be able to postpone gratification and to tolerate the frustrations inherent in this kind of therapy.

By contrast, in the various supportive psychotherapies, the therapist does satisfy some of the patient's needs directly. He is accepting, non-critical, and unabashedly interested in the patient's problems. He is empathic; he may say to the patient: "Yes, I think I can understand what you must be going through." Generally, he also participates more actively in the therapy. He may help the patient to recognize and to delineate the problem; he may give the problem a name and thereby make it less frightening; he may select one aspect of the problem for concentrated therapeutic attention. He may also offer verbal encouragement, or praise, or information; he may set limits to the patient's behavior; rarely, he may even give advice. Satisfying some of the patient's needs in therapy, however, is not an end in itself. It is rather a beginning, a pump-priming, as it were. The final goal is the same as in insight therapy: that the patient will ultimately be able to obtain greater satisfaction from life outside of therapy and be able to dispense with therapy altogether.

The real difference between the two types of therapy is not that one is better than the other. It is a matter of what the patient can tolerate. Sometimes it happens that after a period of supportive therapy a patient can shift to more insight-directed therapy when at the beginning of treatment this would have been impossible. At other times insight therapy is begun and midway in therapy it becomes apparent that the patient cannot endure the frustrations involved. A switch in technique is then indicated. For this reason it is desirable that therapists be skilled in both types so that they can shift techniques as the strengths and the resources of their patients vary.

Psychoanalysis

Psychoanalysis is a system of psychological treatment developed by Freud around the turn of the century (10). Psychoanalysis is also a general psychological theory, but we will not concern ourselves with that aspect of it here. Psychoanalysis is the most intensive, extensive, and expensive form of psychotherapy practised. It is a form of insight therapy. It makes high demands on the patient, and there is general agreement that only a small portion of patients are suitable candidates for psychoanalysis, for some of the reasons which we have already pointed out in the last section. In psychoanalysis, patient and therapist meet for an hour four or five times a week, generally over a period of years, varying from one to five years, and occasionally longer. The patient usually lies on a couch, while the therapist sits behind the patient and out of his view. The patient is instructed to say whatever comes to his mind, no matter how unimportant or strange his thoughts may seem to him. The patient talks, and the analyst listens and occasionally breaks in with a clarifying question. On the whole, however, it is felt that whatever is important to the mental life of the patient will be brought up by him eventually, and that he, not the therapist, is the best judge of what is important to him. In a word, the patient is given considerable responsibility for the pace and direction of his treatment. The therapist for his part will try to discover general themes and patterns of thoughts, and will also try to discern how present behavior relates to the patient's past experience. If he can see such a connection, let us say, between an important event in the patient's childhood and some aspect of his present behavior, he may share this insight with the patient. Technically, this is called making an interpretation. Interpretations can be of many kinds, explanatory, clarifying, comparative, or causal (2). In all instances, however, the therapist is trying to bring to the patient's conscious attention facts and relationships which he perhaps once knew but no longer holds in awareness. Resistance to change occurs in psychoanalysis as it does in other types of psychotherapy. But in psychoanalysis the specific form of the resistance (for instance, every time the analyst makes an interpretation, the patient says: "Yes, I thought you would say that") becomes subject to scrutiny and to further analysis.

In the same way, feelings and thoughts which the patient invariably develops about the therapist are subjected to analysis. Patients are often particularly reluctant to admit to these feelings which to them seem disproportionate and hard to justify. The reason they are hard to understand is that they do not actually relate to the analyst but reflect feelings for and relationships with important other persons in the patient's life, both past and present. The patient's feelings and ways of relating to other people are *transferred* onto the analyst, so to speak. In order not to interfere with the free development of these feelings, the analyst's personality remains in the background and is kept neutral as much as possible. Once the patient has become aware of such feelings and has been able to talk about them, then they are further analyzed and traced back to their origin. In this process two techniques are particularly useful, free association and dream analysis (11, 12). Free association is simply a matter of the patient's saying whatever comes to his mind in connection with what has just been brought up in therapy. It is a way of circumventing the usual conscious control of what is said, and it can thereby reveal deeper layers of the personality. Dream analysis is a second, no less important, way of discovering unconscious wishes and motivations, and Freud called it the "royal road to the unconscious." These two techniques are often used in connection with one another. Dreams are distorted representations of wishes and feelings. Free association to the various elements of the dream can reveal the underlying meaning of the dream's contents.

Much more could be said about psychoanalysis, but since the intent of this book is to provide a brief overview, we will go no further than to present an excerpt from a psychoanalytic hour with a neurotic patient. The vignette illustrates some of the features of psychoanalysis which we have been discussing. The patient is a married woman in her twenties who has been coming for treatment for about three months:

PATIENT: "You know, you remind me a lot of my father."
ANALYST: "Oh?"
PT.: "Yes, you're just like him; I mean in some ways. He used to smile at me like that, like you do when you say 'Hello,' but he didn't mean it. He was just teasing me, just laughing at me, I guess."
AN.: "Laughing at you?"
PT.: "Yes, I guess he thought I was kind of ridiculous. He used to tell stories about me to make other people laugh. I hated it. I used to get so mad I'd cry and throw a fit, and then he'd come over to me and make up and he'd buy me an ice-cream cone. And he used to say I was the best little boy-girl he ever had. You see I was an only child and my father wanted a boy. You know, that's funny. I had a dream the other night, just about that. Only this time it was Ray, you know, my husband, who was buying me an ice-cream cone. Only there was some-

thing funny about how he looked, I can't explain—it was like his hair was turning gray around the temples and Ray's got black hair."

AN.: "When you think of someone with gray hair, who comes to mind?"

PT.: "You, I guess. Now isn't that funny, now I'm starting to have dreams about you."

BEHAVIOR THERAPY

In the last fifteen years a new form of psychotherapy has made its appearance which differs substantially from therapies which we have discussed up to now. It is remarkable in two ways. First, the results obtained with it have been more favorable than with other methods of therapy, with improvement reported in about 90 per cent of cases, compared with the usual 60 to 70 per cent. Second, it is the only therapy for which an experimental basis exists; that is, laboratory experiments with animals can be set up which closely approximate behavior therapy with humans. This is the basis for the claim that behavior therapy is more scientific than other forms of psychotherapy. Behavior therapy is an outgrowth of the work on conditioning by the American psychologist J. B. Watson and the Russian physiologist Ivan Pavlov. Neurotic behavior, particularly neurotic anxiety, is seen as caused by faulty conditioning, and therapy therefore consists of deconditioning techniques. One of the most important of these is *reciprocal inhibition* (13). The principle of reciprocal inhibition is that two differing responses to a stimulus situation (e.g. fear and relaxation, anxiety and anger, panic and co-ordinated motor activity) cannot take place at the same time, and that the occurrence of one will inhibit the other. This principle is used therapeutically in the treatment of neurotic conditions, particularly of phobias and of chronic anxiety states. The patient is systematically taught to give an anxiety-inhibiting response whenever he encounters a previously anxiety-producing situation. Responses which have been used are: deep muscle relaxation (this can be taught or be hypnotically induced), self-assertive verbal statements, and vigorous co-ordinated motor responses. Thus far behavior therapy has not found application in the treatment of psychotic conditions. Its value in the treatment of long-standing personality disorders has also not been fully explored.

There are many other forms and systems of psychotherapy. They cannot all be presented here, but a number of excellent books are available to the reader who wants more thorough-going knowledge in this area (14, 15, 16, 17).

The Limitations of Psychotherapy

Jonathan Swift said that you can't make a silk purse out of a sow's ear. Crude as this expression may seem when applied to psychotherapy, it nevertheless is relevant in setting goals for patients in therapy. A thorough assessment of the patient's level of social and emotional functioning and of his capacity for change is indicated at the beginning of therapy. It can be demoralizing to the patient as well as to the therapist if goals are set too high and consequently cannot be reached. It may be better to start with somewhat more limited goals which can then be increased as progress is made. In general one can expect changes in degree, rather than in direction. Thus one might expect very immature persons to become somewhat more mature as a result of therapy, socially isolated persons to become somewhat more sociable, very dependent persons to become somewhat more independent, or very paranoid persons to become more trusting. A thorough-going personality reorganization is usually not possible, and more limited goals can be accepted as thoroughly worthwhile.

References

1. *Random House Dictionary of the English Language,* unabridged edition, Random House, New York, 1966.
2. Kenneth M. Colby, *A Primer for Psychotherapists,* Ronald Press, New York, 1951.
3. Jerome D. Frank, *Persuasion and Healing,* Johns Hopkins Press, Baltimore, 1961.

4. Ian Stevenson, "The Challenge of Results in Psychotherapy," *Amer. J. Psychiat.*, 116:120–23, 1959.

5. H. J. Eysenck, "The Effects of Psychotherapy: An Evaluation," *J. Consult. Psychol.*, 16:319–23, 1952.

6. A. K. Shapiro, "The Placebo Effect in the History of Medical Treatment: Implications for Psychiatry," *Amer. J. Psychiat.*, 116:298–304, 1959.

7. Franz Alexander and Thomas M. French, *Psychoanalytic Therapy*, Ronald Press, New York, 1946.

8. Sigmund Freud, "Beyond the Pleasure Principle," in *Complete Psychological Works*, Vol. XVIII, edited by James Strachey, Hogarth Press, London, 1947.

9. Sidney Tarachow, *An Introduction to Psychotherapy*, International Universities Press, New York, 1963.

10. Sigmund Freud, *The Origins of Psycho-Analysis*, edited by Marie Bonaparte, Anna Freud, and Ernst Kris, Basic Books, New York, 1954.

11. Franz Alexander, *Psychoanalysis and Psychotherapy*, W. W. Norton, New York, 1956.

12. Sigmund Freud, *The Interpretations of Dreams*, translation by James Strachey, Basic Books, New York, 1955.

13. Joseph Wolpe, *Psychotherapy by Reciprocal Inhibition*, Stanford University Press, Stanford, Calif., 1958.

14. Donald H. Ford and Hugh B. Urban, *Systems of Psychotherapy*, John Wiley, New York, 1963.

15. Paul A. Dewald, *Psychotherapy*, Basic Books, New York, 1964.

16. Frieda Fromm-Reichmann, *Principles of Intensive Psychotherapy*, University of Chicago Press, Chicago, 1950 (also available in paperback, University of Chicago Press, 1960).

17. Carl R. Rogers, *On Becoming A Person*, Houghton Mifflin, Boston, 1961.

11

The Healthy Personality, Its Range and Scope

We have talked a good deal of disease and disorder. It is now time to turn our attention to the more positive aspects of the human personality. In considering the healthy personality it is not sufficient to describe it merely as "freedom from symptoms" or "freedom from neurosis." A search must be made to define it more positively; we want to describe its contours, its texture, and its range of motion. Introducing the topic in this way, we have already indicated that we do not expect the healthy personality to conform to only *one* configuration. Instead, we want to investigate the possible patterns, seek the outer boundaries, the range and scope of the healthy personality. While emphasizing the positive aspects of the healthy personality we will nevertheless find it useful to make frequent comparisons with features found in the neurotic or disordered personality.

Some Criteria of the Healthy Personality

Workers in the field have tried to arrive at some global, shorthand definitions of the healthy personality. Some important criteria and their proponents are listed (1–10).

Successful adaptation to an average expectable environment (Hartmann).

The ability to love and to work (*lieben und arbeiten*) (Freud).
Predominance of conscious and preconscious motivations over
unconscious motivations in one's behavior (Kubie).
Self-realization and productivity (Fromm).
Positive and well-integrated self-concept which corresponds to
reality (Erikson).

All of these are valuable criteria, yet any one taken alone does
not amount to a well-rounded representation of what we are
talking about. Taken together and elaborated upon, however,
they do add up to some useful notions about our subject. In short,
we are saying that a *multidimensional view of the well-functioning personality is in order.*

The Adaptational Approach

Taking the adaptational dimension first, we would say that the
primary criterion here is *flexibility*. By this we mean that an
individual has not only a sizable repertoire of well-developed,
more-or-less automatic responses from which to choose in any
given problem situation, but that he also has the capacity to
develop new responses when his present system of responses
proves inadequate. For example, it is not necessary to develop a
new response every time we approach a red traffic light—the
habitual application of the brakes to bring the car to a halt will
suffice perfectly well; but, when an American prisoner-of-war is
exposed to the stresses of Communist thought reform for the first
time, no familiar pattern of response exists, and his entire adaptive
system will be challenged and perhaps shaken—entirely new responses must be evolved. Each time that a new situation (usually
much less drastic than the brain-washing experience just mentioned) leads to the establishment of a new type of adaptive
response, the over-all effectiveness of adaptation is thereby improved. In other words, a *crisis* in adaptation represents both a
challenge (danger) as well as an *opportunity*.

The adaptational point of view further holds that it is within the scope of the well-functioning personality to be thrown into turmoil and disequilibrium in response to crisis situations. It values more highly the ability *to re-establish equilibrium* than it does the ability *to maintain equilibrium*. These remarks should disabuse anyone of the notion that the healthy person is necessarily tranquil, serene, and therefore, dull. The adaptational approach implies richness, variation, and evolution, not rigidity and stagnation. Furthermore, adaptation is not something which is accomplished once and for all; it is a *continuing* process.

"Lieben und Arbeiten"

When Freud was asked what a healthy person should be able to do, he is reported to have said, "Lieben und arbeiten" (To love and to work). Simple as this criterion may sound, it is yet far-reaching and widely inclusive. This formula, if it can be called that, makes no mention, however, of a third, perhaps equally important area of human behavior—play. Perhaps this omission merely reflects Freud's sober and workmanlike approach to life; perhaps, some might argue, he subsumed play activity (*spielen*) under the capacity for love. Huizinga and others, however, have felt that play activity is a separately definable yet integrally related part of human behavior: *Homo ludens* can take his place beside *Homo faber* (11, 12). In the clinic and in our social contacts, perhaps especially among physicians, we not infrequently see persons who perform well in their work, who have close and loving relationships with their families and who yet are unable to make use of leisure time comfortably. With an ever shorter work week for large numbers of people and with earlier retirement (with its more-or-less enforced leisure), man's ability or inability to play will feature an ever increasing role in his over-all mental health. Therefore as an amendment to Freud's neat formula, instead of "Lieben und arbeiten," we would suggest: "Lieben, arbeiten, und spielen."

Consciousness of Motivation

Freud, in elucidating unconscious motivations, laid the ground work for Kubie's formulation about the healthy personality (6). Kubie feels that to the extent to which we understand why we do something, to that extent are we healthy. He labels behavior of whose motivation we are unaware as neurotic. For example: a young man has just been promoted to an executive position in his firm, a goal for which he has been striving for some time. Instead of feeling pleased and satisfied, as might be expected, he feels depressed, irritable, and disgruntled instead; in addition he has developed a gnawing pain in his stomach. He does not know why he is feeling this way. In fact, this is not the first time he has felt this way in response to seemingly good news: he felt depressed when he was promoted from private to corporal in the army. He again felt bad when he was the only one in his family to have a college education. He may wonder about his paradoxical response but he does not understand it. He is not aware that he is deeply conflicted over his wishes to remain dependent and relatively irresponsible, although his announced intentions are all in the direction of achieving success and independence. A hidden part of himself knows that in accepting the more responsible position he is giving up the security of having other people make decisions for him without having to take responsibility himself. His reaction is then no longer paradoxical but may now be viewed as a reasonable response to a loss which he has incurred. Another person, not similarly conflicted, on a similar occasion might respond to the news of his promotion with delight; he might call his wife and several of his friends to tell them the good news, and perhaps in the evening have a small party to celebrate his promotion. Kubie speaks of *predominance* of conscious over unconscious motivations. We all are governed to some extent by unconscious drives and aims. It is only when major portions of our daily lives are ruled by motives of whose nature and strength we are unaware, that we can no longer consider our personalities to be functioning smoothly.

Self-Realization

Both Fromm and Jung have spoken a good deal of the need or the desirability of self-realization. They feel that lives which are not in congruence with an individual's basic predisposition (temperament, talent, predominant mode of interaction) will result in failures in living and lead either to unhappiness or to symptom formation. When this occurs, efforts in therapy are directed toward discovering the individual's basic personality type and helping him to bring his life goals and activities in alignment with it (9). Fromm and Jung differ in that Fromm emphasizes man's relationship to the society in which he lives, while Jung focuses more on conflicts among the various parts of the self. It should be appreciated that "self-realization" is a term which permits of highly subjective interpretations and regarding which there may be considerable disagreement among observers. Important as subjective factors are in human psychology, this fact again underscores the need for regarding this problem from more than one angle.

Ego Identity

Erikson regards a definite, on the whole positive, ego identity as the cornerstone of the healthy personality structure (2). By ego identity he means a relatively positive concept of oneself, one's position in life, and one's relationships to other people in the environment; a concept which is moreover shared by other people with whom one comes in contact. Faulty or inadequate or negatively valued identity formation may be seen normatively and transiently in adolescence and beginning adulthood and pathologically in nearly all those who seek the help of psychiatrists.

Happiness

To the layman, subjectively felt happiness is an important criterion of healthful living, and a definite goal to be striven for. That so-called happiness may, however, be a mere surface phenomenon should be readily apparent. Certainly, at least until fairly recently, it was often assumed that persons who had become psychotic were in fact happy ("Well, he is happy now"), while nothing could be further from the truth. Similar notions were and are still entertained about the "jolly" fat man and assorted other unhappy persons. In the same vein, people whom we might call pleasure seekers (in our day the "jet-set," but also compare F. Scott Fitzgerald's *Tender Is the Night*) might be regarded as happy on superficial examination, yet this would again constitute a partial, distorted, truth. From a more scientific point of view it may be profitable to regard happiness not as a criterion, but as an epiphenomenon of the healthy personality: a desirable, inevitable, intermittently appearing, by-product of a full life.

References

1. Sidney J. Blatt, "An Attempt to Define Mental Health," *J. Consult. Psychol.*, 28:146–53, 1964.
2. Erik H. Erikson, "Growth and Crisis of the Healthy Personality," in *Transactions* of the Conference on Problems of Infancy and Childhood, Macy Foundation, New York, 1950.
3. Heinz Hartmann, *Ego Psychology and the Problem of Adaptation*, International Universities Press, New York, 1958.
4. Marie Jahoda, "Toward a Social Psychology of Mental Health," in Rose, Arnold M., editor, *Mental Health and Mental Disorder*, Routledge and Kegan Paul, London, 1956.
5. Marie Jahoda, *Current Concepts of Positive Mental Health*, Basic Books, New York, 1958.
6. Lawrence S. Kubie, "The Fundamental Nature of the Distinction Between Normality and Neurosis," *Psychoanalytic Quart.*, 23:167–204, 1954.
7. Frederick C. Redlich, "The Concept of Normality," *Amer. J. Psychother.*, 6:551–69, 1952.
8. Irwin D. Rinder, "New Directions and an Old Problem: The Definition of Normality," *Psychiatry*, 27:107–115, 1964.

9. Anthony Storr, *The Integrity of the Personality*, Pelican Book, 1963, Baltimore, Maryland.
10. John C. Whitehorn, "Guide to Interviewing and Clinical Personality Study," *A.M.A. Arch. Neurol. & Psychiat.*, 52:197–216, 1944.
11. Johan Huizinga, *Homo ludens*, Roy Publishing Co., New York, 1950 (available in paperback from Beacon Press, Chicago.)
12. George Nugent Tyrrell, *Homo faber*, Methuen, London, 1951.

12

The Psychiatric Interview

An interview is a serious conversation between two persons in which the focus of conversation has been deliberately and markedly restricted. Thus it differs from social conversation; yet it is related to it to such a degree that it is often mistaken by the uninitiated for nothing more than ordinary conversation. Good conversationalists, moreover, generally make excellent interviewers if they are trained. Interviewing techniques are used by most physicians to some degree, particularly in taking the medical history. To psychiatrists, interviewing is of especial importance because it is used by them extensively as an evaluation and as a treatment technique.

Interviewing is a skill which can be learned, but it requires a good deal of practice under the close supervision of an experienced interviewer. What is hardest for the beginning interviewer to learn is how to pay attention to not only what the patient is communicating to him but also to what he is communicating to the patient. This dual attention is generally not demanded of the social conversationalist. Interviewing is a technique practised in an interpersonal field; in order for the interviewer to understand fully the interaction, he must be aware of what each of the interactants has contributed.

PURPOSE OF THE PSYCHIATRIC INTERVIEW

The goals of the psychiatrist in a psychiatric interview are not necessarily the same as the patient's. But an interview cannot be successful for either party unless at least some of the goals of both are attained. Otherwise there would be no interaction, and each would go his own way. The goals of the psychiatrist can be stated briefly as follows:

(1) To discover who the patient is and what is troubling him at the moment.

(2) To discover the patient's characteristic patterns of behavior and how these relate to his present difficulties.

(3) To establish a meaningful relationship with the patient which can then facilitate further personality exploration and provide the basis for eventual behavioral change.

The patient might well share these goals with the psychiatrist intellectually. But emotionally he will not rank them first in his hierarchy of values. What he wants from the interview can be stated briefly as follows:

(1) To obtain relief from his suffering.

(2) To make a good impression on the psychiatrist and to be liked by him.

(3) To be told what (outside of himself) is causing his present difficulties.

(4) Lastly, to learn something about himself that might explain his present troubles and prevent future ones.

An interview with a psychiatrist, especially a first interview, is a threatening situation for the patient. We have already mentioned that psychiatric patients generally suffer from low self-esteem, and the mere act of coming to see a psychiatrist has pointed up to them that they are unable to handle their own problems. The psychiatrist should therefore do nothing during the interview which might further undermine the patient's self-confidence. This is no easy task. Also, the likelihood of the psychiatrist's being able to meet the patient's expectations (see above) is slim. But if these expectations cannot be met in full, they can be met to a certain degree. If the patient is unable to obtain complete relief the first session, he may settle for knowing that someone at least understands the nature of his suffering. If he feels that the psychiatrist does not really like him, he will be pleased to find that the psychiatrist at least does not dislike him. He may leave the interview somewhat less distressed than when he came.

If psychiatric patients are anxious about psychiatric interviews, beginning interviewers may also be made anxious by the prospect of interviewing psychiatric patients. This is only natural, due to the newness of the situation. To minimize this anxiety it is helpful for the beginning interviewer to have in mind a rough interview plan. We think the following outline of an initial psychiatric interview is one which can be followed comfortably. It has been found useful in the hands of the author and a goodly number of his teachers and colleagues. It is presented as a guide, to be changed or modified as the interviewer gains experience and develops his own pace and style.

A Suggested Plan for an Initial Psychiatric Interview

(1) *Introduction.* The interviewer introduces himself to the patient and mentions his understanding of the nature and purpose of the interview.

(2) *Beginning to talk.* He then asks the patient, still by way of introduction, to give some simple identifying data—age, marital status, place of employment or place of residence. This serves two purposes. It provides the psychiatrist with some indicators of the patient's probable life experience. It gives the patient an opportunity to begin to talk while yet remaining on emotionally neutral territory.

(3) *Chief complaints.* The patient may by this time have brought up what is troubling him. If he has not done so, it is now time to ask for his complaints. The interviewer will want to hear about these complaints in some detail—exact manifestations, onset, duration, precipitating factors, along with anything else the patient might regard as important or relevant to his problems.

(4) *Past history.* Having gained an appreciation of the patient's present difficulties, the interviewer may turn next to the patient's past life, inquiring particularly into interpersonal relationships, important events, trouble spots, highlights, or previous psychiatric difficulties. The elements and significance of the past history will be discussed further below.

(5) *Summary.* Near the end of the hour the interviewer should summarize for the patient what has been learned about his problems thus far. Such a summary is helpful in itself and also serves as a signal to the patient that the interview is nearly over.

(6) *Course of action and termination.* There remains a course of future action to be decided upon between doctor and patient. This may involve arranging for future appointments, prescription for medication, or referral to another doctor or agency. The patient should also be encouraged to bring up any questions which may have occurred to him. These can then be briefly dealt with, after which the interview is terminated.

The Past History

In order to understand the patient's present psychological functioning, the psychiatrist needs to know a good deal about the patient's past psychological experience and performance. The past is prologue, so to speak. The psychiatrist will therefore gather, during the early stages of his contact with the patient, an extensive personal history. He will particularly emphasize areas of life experience known to be significant in over-all personality development. He will be interested in the specific factual details of the patient's life experience, the specific meaning these experiences had for him, and the psychological response they evoked in him.

Topics To Be Covered in Obtaining a Psychiatric History

1. Family constellation at time of patient's conception.
2. Prenatal, birth, and neonatal history.

3. Milestones of psychomotor development—sitting up, walking, first speech, toilet training.
4. Earliest memories.
5. How does the patient remember his mother? What is his present relationship with her?
6. How does the patient remember his father? What is his present relationship with him?
7. Were there persons other than the patient's parents who took care of him when he was a child?
8. Did he have siblings and how did he relate to them?
9. School history—how he felt about school and how he achieved.
10. Adolescence—how he weathered it.
11. Sexual history—sex education and early experience.
12. Efforts at emancipation from his parents.
13. Job history and military history.
14. Dating and marital history.
15. Medical history.
16. What have been the rough spots in the patient's life?
17. What is his self-image?
18. What are his hopes and aspirations?

These topics need not be approached in this particular order. In fact, to do so might make the gathering of a personal history a somewhat mechanical performance. It is best to allow the patient to chose his own way, indicating to him only broad areas of interest. One would rather run the risk of remaining uninformed about one or more of these areas than to have available an orderly assembly of dry facts which do not further one's understanding of the patient. If a patient has been able to express himself on any significant number of the topics we have mentioned, then very solid groundwork has been laid for future therapeutic interaction between doctor and patient.

Encouraging Patients To Talk Freely

Some patients are able to talk freely, spontaneously, and rele-

vantly about their problems without any particular encouragement from the psychiatrist. But this is the exception rather than
the rule. Many more patients need considerable help to overcome
conscious as well as unconscious barriers to communication. What
are some of these barriers, and what can the psychiatrist do to
facilitate the free flow of information?

Barriers to Communication

To start with, there is the relatively simple barrier of shame or
embarrassment which prevents the patient from speaking of
matters he finds humiliating. This barrier usually drops away as a
relationship is established and as the psychiatrist, by his accepting
and non-critical attitude, proves himself worthy of the patient's
trust.

Next, there is the more complex and more troublesome barrier
of suppression, of consciously holding back. Here the patient is
aware of certain recurring feelings and thoughts which he does
not want to have, which he wants to put out of his mind. These
dark areas are often hinted at by unexplained silences, by circum-
vention, or by outright refusal to discuss certain topics. From the
context the psychiatrist can oftentimes make some perceptive
guesses as to what the patient may be holding back and in so
doing detoxify the threatening area for the patient. He may also
point out that having thoughts and feelings about certain matters
is not the same as acting upon them.

Repression, or unconscious holding back of material, is a formidable barrier to communication. Here the patient is holding
back matters not only from the psychiatrist but from himself.
Slips of the tongue, daydreams, or bits of nonverbal communication (e.g. mannerisms, items of dress) may first point the way
to the hidden material. Specialized techniques, such as free
association or dream analysis, may be needed to fully reveal it.
Making hidden feelings conscious has to proceed hand in hand
with making them acceptable to the patient. Again, the calm,

reassuring, non-judgmental attitude of the psychiatrist can be instrumental.

Learning to interview is in a way a life-long job. New situations arise constantly, a tribute to the infinite variability of human behavior and a challenge to the psychiatrist's equanimity and ingenuity. The topics we have touched on in this chapter will be given amplification and elaboration in the books and articles cited below. But before closing we want to turn a final spotlight on one of the most crucial aspects of the psychiatric interview, its opening moments.

THE FIRST FIVE MINUTES

What happens in the first five minutes of an interview sets the tone for the entire interview, perhaps for the entire interaction between doctor and patient. The patient projects, in condensed fashion, some of the major conflicts and themes which will later be more clearly revealed, much as an overture summarizes in advance the themes in the body of the musical work. It is important, therefore, to pay keen attention to the patient's first statements or acts, his first facial expressions, gestures, and postures. These initial presentations of the patient's self are encapsulations of his basic conflicts, his attitudes toward other people, and his view of himself. Let us give a brief example: A young man enters the psychiatrist's office for the first time. He does not look at the psychiatrist directly or shake his hand. Instead he furtively glances about the office several times, then chooses a seat which is farthest away from the psychiatrist and quite near the door. As the psychiatrist begins to speak, the patient interrupts and says: "I didn't want to come here." As he says so, he pushes his chair farther away from the psychiatrist and puts a hand on the door knob. His entire body tenses and his jaw muscles twitch. At this point the patient has not stated his complaint and no history has been obtained. Yet a tremendous amount of information has already been communicated to the psychiatrist. How the psychiatrist responds will in turn be similarly meaningful to the patient. In this instance the psychiatrist, sensing that the patient feels threatened by any direct approach, turns his chair away from the patient. Speaking quietly and as if to no one in particular, he says: "You know, people who come to a psychiatrist sometimes don't quite know what to expect. Sometimes they get a little scared and almost wished they hadn't come." The patient now lets go of the door knob and relaxes slightly. In barely audible tones he says: "I guess so." The psychiatrist, still not facing the patient, goes on: "Sometimes it is kind of hard to start talking to a stranger." "Yes, I guess so." "But I suppose you do want to tell me what has been bothering you." "Well, I guess so, but, doctor, does anyone else have to know what I tell you?" "No, what you say is between you and me." "Well, you see, my wife and I don't seem to get along anymore. She says I've changed, and maybe I have . . ." The patient is now talking quite freely, and the interview is well under way.

READING LIST ON INTERVIEWING

1. Brian Bird, *Talking with Patients,* Lippincott, New York, 1955.
2. Erik H. Erikson, *Identity and the Life Cycle,* International Universities Press, New York, 1959.
3. Annette Garrett, *Interviewing, Its Principles and Methods,* Family Service Association, New York, 1942.
4. Erving Goffman, *The Presentation of Self in Everyday Life,* Doubleday Anchor Paperback, New York, 1959.
5. Edward T. Hall, *The Silent Language,* Doubleday, New York, 1959 (also available as a paperback, Fawcett World Library, 1961).
6. Ainslie Meares, "Communication with the Patient," *Lancet,* March 26, 1960, 663–7.
7. Ian Stevenson, *Medical History-Taking,* Hoeber, New York, 1960.
8. Harry Stack Sullivan, *The Psychiatric Interview,* Norton, New York, 1954.

Index

GD